Bloom's

GUIDES

Richard Wright's
Native Son

The Adventures of Huckleberry Finn
All the Pretty Horses
Animal Farm
Beloved
Beowulf
Brave New World
The Catcher in the Rye
The Chosen
The Crucible
Cry, the Beloved Country
Death of a Salesman
Fahrenheit 451
Frankenstein
The Glass Menagerie
The Grapes of Wrath
Great Expectations
The Great Gatsby
Hamlet
The Handmaid's Tale
The House on Mango Street
I Know Why the Caged Bird Sings
The Iliad
Jane Eyre

Lord of the Flies
Macbeth
Maggie: A Girl of the Streets
The Member of the Wedding
The Metamorphosis
Native Son
Of Mice and Men
1984
The Odyssey
Oedipus Rex
One Hundred Years of Solitude
Pride and Prejudice
Ragtime
The Red Badge of Courage
Romeo and Juliet
Slaughterhouse-Five
The Scarlet Letter
Snow Falling on Cedars
A Streetcar Named Desire
The Sun Also Rises
A Tale of Two Cities
The Things They Carried
To Kill a Mockingbird
The Waste Land

Bloom's GUIDES

Richard Wright's
Native Son

Edited & with an Introduction
by Harold Bloom

BLOOM'S
LITERARY CRITICISM
An imprint of Infobase Publishing

Bloom's Guides: Native Son

Copyright © 2007 by Infobase Publishing

Introduction © 2007 by Harold Bloom

All rights reserved. No part of this book may be reproduced or utilized in any form or by any means, electronic or mechanical, including photocopying, recording, or by any information storage or retrieval systems, without permission in writing from the publisher. For information contact:

Bloom's Literary Criticism
An imprint of Infobase Publishing
132 West 31st Street
New York NY 10001

ISBN-10: 0-7910-9368-9
ISBN-13: 978-0-7910-9368-9

Library of Congress Cataloging-in-Publication Data
Richard Wright's Native son / Harold Bloom, editor.
    p. cm. -- (Bloom's guides)
  Includes bibliographical references (p.   ) and index.
  ISBN 0-7910-9368-9
  1. Wright, Richard, 1908-1960. Native son. 2. Thomas, Bigger
(Fictitious character) 3. African American men in literature. 4. Trials
(Murder) in literature. 5. Murder in literature. [1. American literature--
History and criticism.] I. Bloom, Harold. II. Title: Native son. III. Series.
  PS3545.R815N3443 2007
  813'.52--dc22   2006037268

Bloom's Literary Criticism books are available at special discounts when purchased in bulk quantities for businesses, associations, institutions, or sales promotions. Please call our Special Sales Department in New York at (212) 967-8800 or (800) 322-8755.

You can find Bloom's Literary Criticism on the World Wide Web at http://www.chelseahouse.com

Contributing Editor: Camille-Yvette Welsch

Cover design by Takeshi Takahashi

Printed in the United States of America

Bang EJB 10 9 8 7 6 5 4 3 2 1

This book is printed on acid-free paper.

All links and web addresses were checked and verified to be correct at the time of publication. Because of the dynamic nature of the web, some addresses and links may have changed since publication and may no longer be valid.

Contents

Introduction

HAROLD BLOOM

Symbolic murders are unacceptable in life, and can be a little hard to take in literature. Before writing *Native Son*, Richard Wright had published a collection of short stories, *Uncle Tom's Children*, which can be regarded as little else but symbolic murders, of whites by blacks, with consequent retributions. Criminal rebellion can be approved as rebellion, when the historical injustices are overwhelming, as they have been and still are for many African Americans. Individual murder is a somewhat different matter, which is one of the reasons why *Native Son* remains so profoundly painful a book. In an earlier introduction to it, I quoted John M. Reilly, a critical follower of Wright, who, in an afterword to an edition of *Native Son*, told us that "the description of Mary's Murder makes clear that the white world is the cause of the violent desires and reactions" that motivated Bigger Thomas to murder Mary Dalton. I remarked in rejoinder, that Wright's novelistic description was quite sufficient to make clear that Bigger Thomas's desires and reactions are somewhat overdetermined, but that he is neither a replicant nor a psychopathic child. He is therefore culpable, if he is a representation of a person and not a mere ideogram.

Eight years of some rather nasty responses to my remarks have not changed my judgment, since those responses detract from the stature of Wright's novel as a novel, rather than a mere social document. Bigger, a Native Son, remains an individual; he suffers and dies as an individual, and he murders as an individual. Wright's narrative strength depends upon Bigger's personal intensity and detailed, naturalistic vividness. The book asks us to comprehend Bigger's hatreds, but surely not to approve of them. As Dan McCall wrote:

> We do not "sympathize" with Bigger. We *feel with* him, perhaps, but we do it in a special way. When Frantz

Fanon speaks of violence, and the necessity for it, he addresses himself to a revolutionary social situation. "Violence" is impelled by consciousness.... Violence is not a helpless reflex, a gross futility, an insane outburst.... But the violent blood baths of Bigger Thomas are at the mercy of the system which engendered them.

Empathy, like sympathy, does not seem the accurate response to Wright's Bigger. He murders Mary because he is driven by hatred of all whites; he murders his own girlfriend, Bessie, who is black, in order to free himself from a filial relationship to her. Like Dostoevsky's Raskolnikov in *Crime and Punishment*, Bigger seeks freedom through the murder of Bessie, thus affirming his own will, yet that seems to me more Richard Wright than Bigger Thomas. The nihilistic aspect of *Native Son* is less persuasive than its Dreiserian, naturalistic element, where Bigger is more at home. He is too desperately blinded by his own hatred and his own dependencies to be judged a nihilist; perhaps more education might have enabled him to quest after such an illusion or given him some inner shield against the self-destructiveness of his own ferocity.

Abdul R. Jan Mohamed, writing on what he calls the "psychopolitical function of death" in Richard Wright's work, asks us to see that violent death, particularly in *Native Son*, serves as a means of escape from "social death," the death-in-life of the slave, or ex-slave, or descendant of a slave still not emancipated by a repressive society. "Psychopolitics" is for me a difficult notion, yet the idea that powerlessness is a "social death" has undoubted force and does provide a somewhat precarious illumination for Wright's most famous book (his autobiography, *Black Boy*, seems to me a larger aesthetic achievement). Theodore Dreiser, Wright's authentic precursor, is similarly illuminated by the idea, and the protagonists of *An American Tragedy* and *Sister Carrie* are after all not slaves or ex-slaves. Dreiser has terrible opacities, but his best novels are redeemed by a massive pathos. *Black Boy* tells us that Wright read Dreiser's *Sister Carrie* and *Jennie Gerhardt*, and they revived in him a vivid sense of his own mother's suffering.

Perhaps *Native Son*, on Marxist grounds, refused to give us such a sense of Bigger Thomas's suffering. Bigger is meant to terrify us, and he does, but Wright has the skill to show us that all too frequently Bigger acts out of intense fear, a realistic terror of the world. Fanon argues that Bigger kills only as a response to the world's expectation that he must kill or die. It is difficult to accept such an argument, in a novel, where almost anything is possible. Richard Wright accepted the aesthetic risk of making Bigger Thomas inarticulate. The risk may have been too great; Bigger goes to his execution in the self-conviction that he is neither better nor worse than most men. A sociopath, to persuade us of that, must be granted eloquence, a certain style of near madness. Wright needed to make his book too harsh for us; we are still so guilty a society that the more humane among us, black and white, feel that we must accept Wright's harshness. If a better time—now nowhere apparent—ever comes in relations between the races in our country, then *Native Son* may yield a place among Wright's books to the more poignant and personal *Black Boy*.

Biographical Sketch

In 1908, Richard Wright was born near Natchez, Mississippi, home to more lynchings than any other state in the union. The grandson of slaves, Wright grew up in the Jim Crow South, destitute after the desertion of his illiterate sharecropper father. Bounced between family, Southern states and orphanages, Wright grew up intimately acquainted with racism: his uncle was lynched for his prosperous business and his mother worked for white families to support herself and her children, though she was often incapacitated by paralytic fits. After graduating as valedictorian of his ninth grade class, Wright moved to Memphis, boarding on Beale Street, a traditionally black neighborhood. Wright quit school after the first few weeks of tenth grade to work a host of menial jobs—porter, dishwasher, factory worker, delivery boy, hall-boy—all in the white world where he felt the racist oppression later illustrated in many of his novels and essays. Wright ardently read Dreiser, Mencken, and Sinclair Lewis during this time. Though libraries refused to loan to him, Wright overcame the problem by using a white man's library card and penning a note that read, "Please let this nigger boy have the following books." He then signed the white man's name and snuck the books home to read.

In December of 1927, Wright and his aunt moved to the South Side of Chicago, where he later set *Native Son*. In 1928, Wright passed a civil service exam after bulking up with a crash diet to achieve the weight minimum—chronic malnutrition had left him thin. He worked for the post office until the Depression forced layoffs and he relied on state support. The relief office gave him a number of jobs, eventually placing him with the WPA Federal Writers' Project which resulted in his first publication, "Superstition," in *Abbott's Monthly*. After a stint selling insurance, Wright joined the John Reed Club where he met a number of Marxists; the exposure resulted in him joining the Communist Party in 1932. As a member of the Party, his writing was valued and appeared in a number of left-wing journals. By May 1937, Wright moved again, this time to

New York to serve as the Harlem editor of *The Daily Worker*. Through it all, he continued to write and in 1938 his first book came out, *Uncle Tom's Children*, a short story collection about racism in the United States Though the book was met with a favorable reception, Wright felt dissatisfied. He thought he had written a book that "even bankers' daughters could read and feel good about." For *Native Son*, he vowed a more aggressive, pitiless book.

Native Son, perhaps Wright's most powerful work, was published by Harper's and selected by the Book of the Month Club for its March installment. Over a quarter of a million copies sold within a month. The responses, though largely favorable, criticized what some critics saw as an overly violent, melodramatic picture of race relations. Others saw it as a wake-up call; Orson Welles opted to work on a stage production with Wright. In 1941, Wright published *Twelve Million Black Voices*, a study of Black migration northward. Three years later, discontent with the Communist Party, Wright left it, articulating his reasons in an article in *The Atlantic Monthly*. Though Wright left the party, the FBI had begun surveillance of his activities in 1943 and did not stop until his death.

Black Boy: A Record of Childhood and Youth was published in 1945, and though it did not sell as widely as *Native Son* did, it still sold well and earned accolades. Still, Wright's discontent with his country was growing; he left for Paris in 1946 at the invitation of the French government. While there, he met Gertrude Stein, Simone de Beauvoir, and other leading French and expatriate intellectuals. In 1947, he permanently left the United States to live abroad. He found himself interested in existentialism and travel. He published *The Outsider* and *Savage Holiday* in 1953 and 1954, respectively, and traveled Africa's Gold Coast, which he wrote about in *Black Power*. He continued writing, this time with a collection of essays, *White Man, Listen!* (1957). His final novel, *The Long Dream*, was published in 1958 though an early novel, *Lawd Today!* was published posthumously.

In 1960, Wright suffered a heart attack in Paris. He was cremated, with a copy of *Black Boy*, and interred at Paris's famous Père Lachaise cemetery. Even in death, he never returned to the United States, though he found a great following in the 1960's with the Black Power movement. His work will long be studied for its literary, sociological, and historical importance.

The Story Behind the Story

When *Uncle Tom's Children* went into print, it was widely applauded by audiences, black and white, not a result that Wright had intended. With his next book, he wanted to return to issues of race, oppression and violence, but he wanted to do so in such a way as to unsettle the status quo rather than write a book about which white people might feel self-righteous. He claimed, "no one would weep over it; that it would be so hard and deep that they would have to face it without the consolation of tears."

In 1940, Richard Wright wrote "How Bigger Was Born," an essay in which Wright closely examined his own modes of creation. Through this analysis, Wright offers a fairly extensive view of the creation of the character and the book itself. He also outlines many of the themes and structures of the book, giving readers insight into the story behind the story.

He begins the essay by tracing the origins of Bigger through a series of boys and men he knew in his youth and young adulthood. Each character defies Jim Crow, demands what he wants, lives by violence, and for many, either dies by violence or is incarcerated because of it. He wrote of Bigger No. 1, "[H]is life was a continuous challenge to others. At all times he *took* his way, right or wrong, and those who contradicted him had him to fight. And never was he happier than when he had someone cornered and at his mercy; it seemed that the deepest meaning of his squalid life was in him at such times." While Bigger No. 1 only understood violence, Bigger No. 2 could articulate nothing other than his hatred for whites. Bigger No. 3 brutalizes his own race for personal gain and Bigger No. 4 does nothing save lament the idea that "white folks won't let us do nothing." Bigger No. 5, who refuses to sit at the back of the bus and uses racial stereotypes to his own advantage, claiming he can't read the sign assigning him a seat, is the only Bigger to inspire pride in his fellow black men. Bigger Thomas became a composite of the many men who acted against the limits of a racially oppressive society.

In 1934, Wright worked at the South Side Youth Club in Chicago with rebellious, black, urban youth. He hated the job and felt insulted and disgusted by the idea that ping pong tables and checkers might keep the boys in check after the realities of their lives. In "How Bigger was Born," he writes of hoping that the boys would leave the shelter and inflict some mayhem on the white property surrounding the Black Belt. He wrote "that was the only way I could contain myself for doing a job I hated; for a moment I'd allow myself, vicariously, to feel as Bigger felt—not much, just a little, just a *little*—but still, there it was." The experience forced Wright to face his own fears and desires.

While he wanted to write, he also feared the responses of both white and black America. He imagined the whites to be appalled, to believe the book espouses hatred, which critic David L. Cohn stated in *Atlantic Monthly*. He imagined the Black community, particularly the upper-middle class of doctors and professionals, would find the book offensive and question why Wright would put forth such a negative stereotype when he had the opportunity to write something uplifting about the race. Wright himself had to break free from the potential for self-censorship embodied by those imagined critics. He claims that the novel became necessary in order that he might "free [him]self of this sense of shame and fear." The writing became an almost violent act, one which would burst on to the literary and political scene as a book-of-the-month club selection, an event which propelled sales.

Many critics believe, and certainly *Black Boy* attests to this, that much of Bigger's experience comes from that of Wright himself. Because Wright lived in Chicago's South Side, he could render the city as an overwhelming presence in the book. Because he experienced tension in a tiny apartment with a demanding family headed by a religious zealot matriarch, he can imagine Bigger's mother and siblings. Because he read closely the newspapers filled with lurid tales of racial crimes, particularly that of Robert Nixon and Earl Hicks, he knew the rhetoric of race in the news. The men were charged with the alleged rape and murder (beaten to death by a brick) of Patricia Johnson. The Chicago Tribune covered the crime with lurid, racist language, calling Hicks "the brick moron," "the jungle beast," "the sex moron," and "racist slayer." He was charged and convicted of rape and murder, though no evidence of rape appeared. The trial lasted a year and ended with Hicks's death. During the trial, the police tried to blame additional crimes on Hicks. For Wright, the trial further proved the necessity of Bigger's story.

It is important to note that in writing *Native Son* Wright spent time brainstorming, trying to construct Bigger in his head. If Wright could imagine Bigger fully, then he knew the inevitable plot. He also limited his point of view to what Bigger could imagine, though that also limited Wright's ability to articulate things in the novel. Nevertheless, he couldn't give the experience of Bigger without that imposed limitation.

The book initially sold over 250,000 copies in the first year, largely due to its place as a Book-of-the-Month Club selection. The influential club also demanded a series of cuts, including the movie theater masturbation scene; Wright obliged them though the scenes have since been reinstated. Though *Native Son* appeared early in Wright's career, none of his later books matched its fury or its popularity.

List of Characters

Bigger Thomas is a twenty-year old African American youth, born in Mississippi, bred in the South Side of Chicago, who kills Mary Dalton and kills and rapes Bessie Mears after years of racial and class oppression. Throughout the book, he is unable to articulate his rage or his belief that through killing and violence he finally gained the ability to make choices in his own life.

Mary Dalton is the daughter of rich white parents, a communist sympathizer, the girlfriend of communist organizer, Jan, and the murder victim of Bigger Thomas. She tries to be sympathetic to Bigger, but in so doing insults and enrages him with her unaccountable behavior. She becomes a symbol of white fear, hatred, and guilt in relation to African Americans.

Bessie Mears is the girlfriend and murder/rape victim of Bigger Thomas. After years as a silent servant to white families, she was coerced into helping Bigger ask for a ransom from the Dalton family—a request she tried to resist though she is the one who inadvertently gave Bigger the idea. She also tells him that killing a white woman, regardless of the numbers of black people killed, is still wrong. Her death is nearly forgotten in respect to Mary's, illustrating the relative concern given to crimes by blacks against blacks versus crime by a black man against a white woman.

Buddy Thomas is the younger brother of Bigger Thomas. Together with their mother and sister, they occupy a tiny, rat-infested apartment. Buddy looks up to Bigger, and after Bigger's arrest offers to commit crimes to aid his brother, bringing about the realization in Bigger that his crimes are larger than himself.

Vera Thomas is the younger sister of Bigger Thomas. She fights with her brother constantly, often taking the side of her mother in accusing Bigger of being lazy and unmanly. At the novel's end, her fear and love for him make Bigger realize the pain that he has caused his family.

Mrs. Thomas is Bigger's mother and a great influence on his self-worth. Because he has no job, she considers him less than a man and claims that she wishes he had never been born. After his arrest, she sends a preacher to his cell to bring him back to Christianity, hoping that God will save him. Wright uses her to illustrate the important role of Christianity among some poor African Americans.

Mr. Dalton is the rich, white businessman for whom Bigger goes to work. He is the father of Mary Dalton and a philanthropist who gives money to the NAACP while simultaneously charging inflated rents to African American families through his South Side Real Estate Company.

Mrs. Dalton is the blind wife of Mr. Dalton and mother to Mary. She offers to send Bigger to school to better himself. Wright uses both her and her husband to represent the often ineffectual and hypocritical attempts of white America to help underprivileged African Americans. She is also present in the room when Bigger kills Mary, although she is unable to see him.

Jan Erlone is a Communist organizer and the boyfriend of Mary Dalton. He believes that all men are equal regardless of race and forces Bigger to socialize with him and Mary. Bigger tries to use him as a patsy for the crime, betting on the public's negative associations with the Communist party. After Bigger's arrest, Jan tries to help him by bringing Max to defend him.

Boris A. Max is a Jewish lawyer who becomes the object of hatred by the angry mob of white people screaming for the death of Bigger. He is a member of the Communist party and the only true friend Bigger has in the novel. He presents the "race question" in his defense, suggesting that the circumstances of racial hatred and oppression as well as class created the killer in Bigger.

Jack Harding, G.H., and **Gus** are members of Bigger's gang of friends. Together, they rob black businesses, play pool, imitate white people, and plan a burglary of a white business. Terrified that they will be caught for the crime, Bigger goads Gus into a fight to keep them from following through on the plan. Gus identifies the action as resulting from Bigger's fear and hatred. The boys later visit Bigger in jail and testify to his sanity.

Doc is the owner of the pool hall in which Bigger fights Gus and destroys a pool table. He testifies at the hearing as to Bigger's sanity.

Buckley is the white state's attorney, a racist, anti-Communist bent on getting the death penalty for Bigger. He uses the media and the courtroom as a forum to incite public hatred against Bigger, blacks, Communists and non-Christians and to get himself re-elected based on that feeling.

Britten is the white detective who hounds Bigger in the initial hours after Mary's death. Mr. Dalton convinces the detective to leave Bigger alone. He later appears at the hearing, testifying to Bigger's sanity.

Reverend Hammond is the preacher from Mrs. Thomas's church. He comes to the jail to convince Bigger to pray for salvation in the next life. Bigger refuses his offer and sees the man as ridiculous—one given the drug of religion to forget the injustices with which he lives.

Peggy is the white, Irish housekeeper who associates herself with the family in a way that Bigger never can.

Summary and Analysis

I. Fear

Aptly, *Native Son*'s first chapter proclaims the single greatest underlying fact of the life of Wright's protagonist: fear. The emotion colors nearly every interaction Bigger Thomas has, whether he is actively in fear and running for his life, or simply considering the consequences of being black in certain neighborhoods. Every negative moment in Bigger's life is compounded by fear. Wright begins in scene, with the Thomas family—sister Vera, brother Buddy, and mother Mrs. Thomas—asleep and waking suddenly to the alarm. The furniture of the apartment consists of two iron beds and a kitchenette with chairs. So cramped is the space that the boys must turn their heads to allow the women to dress, then the women must do the same to allow the boys to dress. Physically, there is no room for separation from the other, and that closeness breeds mental resentment and a desire to be invisible, to spend a moment unseen. Unfortunately, for an African American living in Chicago, racism is a visual stigma, making it nearly impossible to hide.

As the women dress, a large black rat races into the room. Immediately, the women panic, and Bigger as the eldest son and man of the house must take on the interloper and protect his family. The story begins with violence as Bigger chases and kills the rat, but the moments before the rat's demise set up a powerful parallel with Bigger's later bouts with the law and the facts of his life in the South Side of Chicago. Trapped, the rat runs in circles, then, unable to see a way out, he tries to strike out in violence though the attempt is futile. Like Bigger, he is struck down; his death, part of everyday life in the city, as Wright illustrates, is the death of black men.

Notably, Bigger strikes the head of the rat. The destruction of the head is a pattern to follow throughout the novel, perhaps because racism exists in the perception of the person rather than in the reality of the world. To destroy that perception, Bigger repeatedly attacks the head, the place of judgment.

After killing the rat, Bigger picks it up by its tail and swings it before Vera, who becomes so terrified she faints. Many critics have looked at Wright's treatment of women in his novels, citing misogynistic tendencies. Here, Vera presents Bigger with a rare opportunity—she is someone with even less power than him. In 1938 Chicago, any white person would be considered better than a black man, but a black man is still more powerful than a black woman. Eager to take his frustration out on someone, Bigger often turns to those weaker than him, particularly the black women in his life.

After scaring his sister into a faint, Bigger takes the rat outside, and when he returns his mother begins her attack—an attack that Wright implies is habitual. She says, "Boy, sometimes I wonder what makes you act like you do," and "Bigger, sometimes I wonder why I birthed you." Bigger responds suggesting maybe she should have just left him unborn, expressing openly his dissatisfaction with his life. Wright also introduces the word "black" into the story as an adjective used by the family, to describe someone's attitude. His mother, referring to Bigger, says "He's just crazy ... Just plain dumb black crazy." The word evolves over the course of the novel. When used by the black characters to talk about each other, the word is used to indicate social circumstance, a culmination of life as people trapped in the South Side. Rarely is it used to simply indicate the actual color. When white people use it, it often refers to the same social straits and assumptions.

Bigger and his mother begin to argue about the job offered by welfare. The rich, white Daltons have offered, through social services, to hire Bigger as a chauffeur. Were Bigger to refuse, the family would lose their housing. His mother defines his taking the job as his duty as a man, one of the few traits of a man allowed him, but it is hollow as it offers him little respect or opportunity to fulfill his potential. The job as servant only antagonizes Bigger's sense of his very limited world. Vera readies herself for sewing school so that she will have a trade, and Mrs. Thomas prepares for another day of washing, repeating over and over again how exhausted she is. Bigger tries to resist their pathos and Wright explains Bigger's need for distance:

> He knew that the moment he allowed himself to feel to its fullness how they lived, the shame and the misery of their lives, he would be swept out of himself with fear and despair. So he held toward them an attitude of iron reserve; he lived with them, but behind a wall, a curtain. And towards himself he was even more exacting. He knew that the moment he allowed what his life meant to enter fully into his consciousness, he would either kill himself or someone else. So he denied himself and acted tough (10).

The result of his denial is a disconnection with his family and even his own emotions; the disconnect also provides fertile ground for his own hatred to stew unappeased. Wright provides, in this first scene, ample foreshadowing for the events which follow. Feeling oppressed by his mother and the needs of his family, he eats quickly, takes the last bit of money his mother has, and leaves the apartment, moving into the city to look for some freedom of activity and thought.

Still, once he is in the streets, he realizes that he has very little money and thus few options for amusement as he must save fourteen of his twenty-six cents to get to the Daltons' house. He imagines himself out of his predicament with the burglary of Blum's Delicatessen. With his friends, G.H., Gus, and Jack, he has plotted but never gone through with the idea, primarily because Blum is white. The young men committed petty crimes around the neighborhood but never against a white victim. The very fact of whiteness, in Bigger's world, made the crime real, something the police could not simply ignore as they could with black crimes against blacks. After a few moments, his friend, Gus, meets with him on the street corner. Together they share a smoke, watch passing cars and women, and consider what they would do if they were white, rich, and educated. Every dream is filled with so many 'ifs' that they break into angry laughter. Were Bigger to fly, he claims he would drop bombs. The candor with which Wright portrayed the bitterness of Bigger and Gus shocked white audiences. They continue their conversation, doing their best impressions of 'important' white men. Able mimics, their play is fast-paced, smart and bitter, but also full of distance. The white world seems far away and the boys examine whites with some of the critical awe of an anthropologist, noting behaviors and customs. Bigger claims to know phrases and conversation styles from the movies, not from experience—an early nod to the influence of media on popular perception. As they continue their play, the exchange fills with the hatred between races, ending finally in a bitter exclamation from Bigger, "They don't let us do *nothing*." Bigger cannot resign himself to the idea. He tells Gus:

> I know I oughtn't think about it, but I can't help it. Every time I think about it I feel like somebody's poking a red-hot iron down my throat. Goddammit, look! We live here and they live there. We black and they white. They got things and we ain't. They do things and we can't. It's just like living in jail. Half the time I feel like I'm on the outside of the world peeping in through a knothole in the fence.

Bigger continues to tell Gus that he fears that "something awful" is going to happen to him, or as he says later, that he will do something awful. Gus advocates denial and repression, for Bigger to stop thinking about all the inequality, but it festers in Bigger and cannot be ignored. The two head to the poolroom where they meet up with G.H. and Jack. There Bigger reintroduces the plan to burglarize Blum's. The other men protest but Bigger insists on the plan, calling them cowards until they reluctantly agree. Gus is the last holdout, scared of committing a crime against a white man as is Bigger. But Bigger needs the moment to prove something, to act. Still, Gus is the biggest threat because he understands and shares Bigger's fear; he is the one who can't be bluffed. When Gus calls him out, Bigger responds with fury, wanting to hurt Gus for making him feel afraid and small. G.H. and Gus leave the poolroom to give Bigger time to calm down. Jack tells Bigger that they can't pull a job off if they're fighting, which Bigger acknowledges. To calm down, they head to the movies to see *Trader Horn*, a movie largely filmed in Africa and where the hero is constantly fighting against cannibalistic "savages." It reinforces many racist stereotypes concerning Africa and its people.

Jack and Bigger sit in the darkness together, masturbating, racing to see who will finish first, and claiming they wished their girls were there. Bigger even jokes that if a woman passing them returned to see what they were doing, he would rape her. It illustrates much of Bigger's misogyny and his belief about the place of women in his life. When they finally reach release, they step over their mess and head to other seats where they sit working out the details for the Blum job. The Book-of-the-Month Club asked for the expulsion of the masturbation scene though it is later used in the trial to illustrate Bigger's sexual ferocity as it relates to the alleged rape of Mary Dalton.

The newsreel that begins the movie introduces Bigger to Mary Dalton for the first time as he and Jack watch her cavort around the beach with her Communist boyfriend, Jan Erlone. The reel makes clear that she has incurred the displeasure of her family by running off with Jan. Bigger recognizes the name and tells Jack. Together they weave a fantasy where Mary makes advances towards Bigger and becomes his lover, or perhaps, Bigger thinks, she will pay him to help her meet her secret lover. Bigger also dreams that working from the 'inside' he will learn the art of making money from the rich white people. As he fantasizes, *Trader Horn* begins with its images of African peoples dancing to drum music. He ignores that and focuses instead on an image of white America and its amassed wealth. Even in his daydreams, Bigger imagines all wealth, intelligence, and power to be the province of white people. Bigger also realizes that the job might afford him some long sought independence and he begins to regret his decision to encourage the Blum job. After leaving the theater, Jack and Bigger split off to get their guns for the pending robbery.

Terrified of what might happen, Bigger returns to the pool hall to meet his friends.

His tension lessens slightly when he sees that Gus has not yet arrived. In his mind, there still might be time to escape from the situation in which he has placed himself. To boost his confidence, he begins to attack the motives of the absent Gus until he arrives. Then, desperate to avoid the job and its potential consequences, he attacks Gus physically, kicking and beating him and finally holding him down to the ground and making him lick his knife. The humiliation of his friend is reminiscent of the misogyny throughout the book and the way in which power has an almost sexual element for Bigger. Neither his friends nor Doc, the owner, make a move to stop Bigger. By the end of the episode, Bigger declares it too late to attempt the job, thereby extracting himself from the potential situation. Typical of Bigger, when pushed into a corner, like the metaphoric rat, he lashes out. Before fleeing the scene, Jack takes a last swing at Bigger, throwing a pool ball at his head. When it hits, Bigger leaps up to attack his friend but ends up slipping on a pool cue. The men around him laugh, and Bigger reacts with rage, slashing the felt of the table and urging Doc to use his gun. Again, violence is the only way Bigger believes he can restore his pride.

Bigger leaves, walks down the street and starts to laugh. As he laughs, he notices a tear slip down his face and tells himself that he laughed so hard he cried. Bigger is barely cognizant of his own emotional landscape. He returns home, briefly, to his questioning mother, and Wright explains to the reader that "His confused emotions had made him feel instinctively that it would be better to fight Gus and spoil the plan of the robbery than to confront a white man with a gun." Bigger fails to make the connection, instead believing that he was simply punishing Gus for being late. Throughout the novel, the interior life of the character is illuminated to the reader, but not to the character, creating an intense kind of dramatic irony. Bigger never comes to a full understanding of self; circumstances have made that utterly impossible.

At five, his mother pushes him out of the house to see about the job; he keeps his gun with him to stave off his feeling of uneasiness. When he gets to the house, he can't decide whether he is to come in the front or the back of the house, and that confusion fuels his hatred and fear. He heads to the front of the house and is admitted by Peggy, the housekeeper. She seats him and finds Mr. Dalton. Alone in the house of a white man, Bigger grows increasingly uneasy before he is presented to Mr. Dalton. As Dalton examines him, Bigger feels intensely aware of his skin color, his history, his status in the white world. As he stands, Mrs. Dalton, a symbol of ineffectual, wealthy white philanthropy passes, her arms outstretched. Unnerved, Bigger steps back for her wraith-like presence to pass, and sees she is blind. After she leaves, Dalton continues the interview, asking Bigger if he thought he would like driving. Bigger slips into the role of servant, saying "Yessuh" though it is not his normal speech. Horrified by his own behavior, Bigger doesn't know how to stop himself. As the interview progresses, Dalton asks Bigger about his record and makes an affected gesture of forgiveness then offers him a job. As the interview concludes, Bigger meets Mary, the Dalton's young, spoiled daughter, the one from the movie. Immediately, she asks if he belongs to a union, catching him off-guard and adding to the discomfort of the proceedings. When Mr. Dalton steps out to speak to his daughter, Bigger has a flash of intuition—thinking that he needs to leave Mary alone, and that she is crazy and could cause him to lose his job. Unfortunately, she is also his first assignment in the house.

Peggy takes Bigger to the back of the house, feeds him, and settles him into his room, all the while delivering a glowing review of her employers and the former chauffeur, Mr. Green. She tries to use Green, who Mrs. Dalton sent to night school, as an example for Bigger. She shows him how to stoke the furnace and where to find the car. Bigger relaxes a little, for the first time in a room of his own, but Mary remains a source of fear. Bigger heads to the kitchen for water and encounters Mrs. Dalton, who tries to talk to him about education, an agenda she pushes though she has no knowledge of Bigger.

He exits the kitchen and picks up Mary, who directs him to take her not to the intended university lecture but to the Loop to pick up Jan.

Mary questions him to see if she can trust him; she claims she is on his side, a statement that confounds Bigger until he realizes that she is talking about Communism. Mary continues to talk to him and ask him questions about "his people," illustrating her ignorance and her distance from him. Both she and Jan, though they want to be open, have a "look at the aborigines" attitude when it comes to their interaction with Bigger. One moment he is a comrade, and the next he is a servant who must obey them. When Bigger first meets him, Jan insists on a handshake. Bigger tries to refuse, but Jan is determined, forcing Bigger to break the unspoken laws about white people. Mary recognizes his reluctance to call Jan by his first name, then patronizingly tells him, "It's all right, Bigger," she said, "Jan *means* it." Suddenly, Bigger has no idea what to do and the job, which should have been simple, becomes very complicated. If he doesn't comply with their orders to befriend them, will he be fired? If he is too friendly, will he be fired? If he is seen, will he be fired, particularly when Jan decides to drive, putting Bigger between Mary and him in the front seat, depriving him of his purpose in being there?

He holds himself tightly in the car, trying not to touch either of them, as Jan and Mary exclaim over the beauty of the city. They ask Bigger to recommend a restaurant, saying they want to see how the people really live in the South Side. He reluctantly agrees, and finds himself dining publicly with them in an all black restaurant. He sees his girl, though he rebuffs her, not wanting her engaged in the ensuing debacle. Jan and Mary play at adopting black language and Jan launches into an interrogation of Bigger. By the end of the conversation, Jan and Mary offer to be friends with Bigger. A few comments later, Mary asks Bigger if he will carry her trunk and drive her to the train the next morning. One minute, the couple is trying to be friends, the next they revert to treating Bigger like a servant and talking about black people as a monolith. In one of the book's most excruciating moments, Mary exclaims,

"They have so much *emotion*! What a people! If we could ever get them going ..." Jan responds that revolution can't happen without them. Drunk, Mary urges Bigger to sing Swing Low, Sweet Chariot." He refuses, and Mary and Jan begin to sing themselves, earning Bigger's derision. They ask him to drive around while they have relations in the back. Afterwards, Bigger drops Jan off and returns home with the very drunk Mary, who he helps up the stairs into her bedroom. Once there, she lolls on the bed, and Bigger, attracted to her body, begins to sexually molest her, kissing her and feeling her breasts. Drunk and half-asleep, Mary responds and Bigger intensifies his attentions until he hears Mrs. Dalton whisper at the door. Terrified, Bigger stills, then covers Mary's face with a pillow to keep her quiet. He continues pushing the pillow down, knowing that if he is found he will not only lose his job but will likely be charged with rape due to prevailing racist notions about black men's insatiable desire for white women. Backed into a corner, he again responds with violence, suffocating the struggling girl. Her mother hears the struggle and comes closer, realizing as she does that she can smell alcohol. Worried and disappointed, she assumes the girl is drunk and leaves the room. Bigger sinks to the floor, flooded with relief until he realizes that he has accidentally killed Mary. Immediately he realizes not only has he killed her, but he, a black man, has killed a white woman—a crime of epic proportion in the public eye.

Bigger constructs a plan; he decides to put the girl's body into her trunk and carry it downstairs, put it in the car, and deliver it to the station, giving him three days of cover with her pending trip. When it is discovered she is lost, he plans to blame Jan, the Communist. The papers included a great deal of anti-Communist rhetoric, much in the same way they enflamed racist rhetoric. Once in the basement, he stares at the furnace, and decides to stuff Mary's body inside it and burn all evidence of the crime. He shoves her body in up to her neck, and decides to cut off her head since it won't fit. He piles newspapers under her neck and attempts to use his knife, but the bone is too strong; he turns to a hatchett and severs the head with one blow. He wraps it in newspaper and throws it into the fire. Exhausted, he carries the trunk to the car and loads it, thinking that delivering it would lessen suspicion. He empties the money from her purse, ready to run away, and heads home, where he falls into a deep sleep, thereby ending section one. In this section all of Bigger's actions are predicated on his fear of white people and persecution. In the next section, Wright explores Bigger's flight from the legal system and from the young man he once was.

II. Flight

Bigger wakes at home, remembering all that had happened the night before. He realizes he left Mary's purse in plain sight. Panicked, he picks up the purse, stuffs his dirty knife inside it, and dresses. He also sees Jan's pamphlets, which he nearly throws away before deciding that they might help to incriminate Jan. He walks out and throws the purse and knife into a garbage can, all the while wondering if Mary's body burned. Back at home, he starts to pack his suitcase, preparing to move to the Dalton's. He is haunted by a vision of Mary's severed head. His mother calls out to him, questioning him about the job and his nervousness. They begin to argue about what time he returned home, and Bigger begins to solidify his alibi with his family, though they are unaware of it.

His mother reminds him that this job is finally his chance, although Bigger knows that even without the events of the previous night it is still a limited chance. He prepares the suitcase, still being questioned by his mother, then by his brother. Bigger becomes increasingly impatient and uneasy as his family insists on the hour of his return. He worries that he will be found out, but his brother's adoration calms him as they talk about his job and his girlfriend, Bessie. As they talk and eat breakfast, Bigger begins to think about what he has done, the magnitude of it—something that matters, whether good or bad. He denies the killing was an accident, believing that his whole life had brought him here; he simply had not had the opportunity in the past. When the circumstances arose, so did the killing instinct, born of oppression, rage, and limitations. In his mind, he has killed before.

Making the action inevitable and nearly intentional gives Bigger a feeling of power. He has finally done something unthinkable, lived up to an awful potential. Unlike those around him, he took action. For good or for evil, he believes his life now means something. As he watches his family, he likens them to blind people—unable to see his will, what he has done, or what life is doing to them. He alone has taken his destiny into his own hands. He thinks that his family, Jan and the Daltons's are blind to the potential within him. He compares his family to Jan and Mary, finding Buddy vague and Vera terrified, so unlike their white counterparts. He sees how they can be manipulated. He leaves after breakfast, and Buddy follows him down the street to give him the roll of Mary's money which has fallen from his pocket. Buddy, concerned that Bigger might be in trouble because of the money, questions his brother, but Bigger reveals nothing, though inwardly he panics, wondering how much he has revealed. He gives Buddy some money then swears him to secrecy.

He continues walking through the snowy city, stopping to see his friends and give them cigarettes bought with his new windfall. He makes up with Gus, then boards a streetcar, where he rationalizes killing Mary, thinking that she made him do it with her behavior, so unlike the actions normally sanctioned between blacks and whites. He worries that he can't get the vision of Mary's severed head out of his mind. As the streetcar progresses to the Dalton's he begins to muse over Hitler, feeling admiration for the solidarity the man created among Germans, wishing that a black man would do that for the black people. When he arrives at the Dalton's, he heads in through the kitchen, nervous and eager to see if anyone has noticed Mary's absence. Peggy tells him to tend the furnace and asks after Mary. Bigger claims he hasn't seen her yet and that she told him to leave the car out overnight. He then heads downstairs to check on the status of Mary's body. Reassured that she burned, he takes the trunk upstairs to continue the diversion and waits for Peggy's interference. Peggy calls for

Mary and when she doesn't hear her, she assumes that Mary stayed somewhere else that night. She begins to question Bigger and he slowly releases information, particularly about the presence of Jan. Confused, Peggy tells Bigger to take the trunk to the station. When he returns, she feeds and questions him, growing increasingly worried. Bigger, on the other hand, grows increasingly confident and begins to feel a sense of equality with the white world. He possesses information and a will that as of that moment, he believes to be unmatched. After breakfast, he returns to his room where he can hear Mrs. Dalton talking to Peggy in the kitchen, asking after Mary. With Jan as a convenient scapegoat, Peggy suggests that perhaps Mary has run off again. Unsatisfied, Mrs. Dalton goes to Mary's room and discovers that half of her traveling clothes are still in her room.

She calls for Bigger, asking him about the trunk and Mary's whereabouts. Bigger relies on her adherence to the servant/master relationship, knowing that she will not want to reveal her worry about Mary to him. She stops questioning him and gives him the day off, ashamed of her daughter's behavior. With the afternoon off, he heads to see Bessie, thinking as he goes that he did not earn enough money for the murder that he should have planned ahead. When he arrives at Bessie's, she plays coy with him, angry that he barely acknowledged her the night before when he showed up at the restaurant with Jan and Mary. She tries to gauge his desire for her by making him explain himself and flirt with her, a game that excites him. The game ends when Bigger shows her his wad of cash. Bessie, who moves between drinking, working and having sex with Bigger, is entranced by the money and its possibilities—marriage, the end of work, escape. Still, she questions where he got it. Bigger doesn't answer; instead, he tells her that he will buy her something and she contents herself with that. Eventually, the two have sex and Bigger feels relaxed until Bessie begins asking him about his job. Suspicious Bigger evades with short answers. She keeps talking about a family whose son was kidnapped and killed; the killers tried to extort money from the family. Bigger is struck by how he might make Mary's death worth something.

He decides to write a ransom note, collect the money, and skip town. Bessie notices his sudden distraction and demands an explanation. The two argue and Bigger begins to see Bessie as blind like his family, and without options and the power to make her own decisions. He sees that theirs is a business deal; he buys her alcohol and she pays with her body. He is torn between affection for the unguarded woman that he sees when they make love and the suspicious, jaded woman he sees when they argue.

The two leave her apartment and head out for a drink. Bessie still wonders what Bigger is up to with his sudden windfall and secrecy. He decides that he can use Bessie to help him but worries that she will be his downfall. So, he plans an elaborate story about Mary eloping with Jan. He explains that they can claim she was kidnapped, collect the money and then leave town without doing any harm to anyone. Bessie claims he's crazy but she continues asking about it. He tries to seduce her with a life in New York, in Harlem, where life is better for black people, where there are possibilities. They leave the restaurant and Bessie continues to worry about getting caught, but Bigger assures her that the police and the family are too racist to believe that black people could commit so thoughtful a crime. Bessie wonders how Bigger is so sure that the girl is gone. Finally, impatient with the discussion, Bigger forces Bessie to make a decision. Bessie barely commits, but he feels sure that she will go along with the plan. He returns to the Dalton house feeling triumphant, as if he finally has some control over his destiny.

He enters the basement, checks the furnace and reminds himself to clean out the ashes and make sure the bones burned. Peggy calls from above, telling him that Mary is missing—the trunk was never picked up and Mary never arrived in Chicago. Bigger feigns surprise, then answers questions posed by the increasingly frantic Mr. and Mrs. Dalton. As planned, he begins to set Jan up for the fall, though Mr. Dalton still believes she has run away, as she has in the past. They send Bigger for the trunk, and on the drive he plots the ransom note and drop place. He will have Bessie waiting in an abandoned building, to get the money. He considers leaving, but he believes that he is in control of the situation and can still make it go his way. He returns with the trunk and finds that a detective, Mr. Britten, has been called onto the case.

Britten embodies much of the learned prejudice Wright fights. From the beginning, he is ready to either blame the black man or the Communist. Completely a product of his time, Britten sees both Bigger and Jan as evil, based on their assigned racial and political designations. He believes that he understands their characters through what he has read in the paper or seen on T.V. When he meets Bigger, Britten makes a point of showing him a badge to assert his power. He begins questioning Bigger about the trunk and the previous night; Bigger sees Britten as himself, scared, angry, aggressive. Bigger decides to use all of the stereotypes about African Americans to his advantage and plays dumb by answering only those questions asked, dropping hints about Jan, and pretending he is protecting the mischievous Mary. As the interrogation continues and Bigger sees his success, he feels flush with power. He is in charge of the story for once, and his story finds Jan guilty. The story slips a little as Britten begins to suspect Bigger of Communist leanings. The questioning gets heated, Britten slams Bigger against the wall and yells, "You *are* a Communist, *you goddamn* black sonofabitch!" In Britten's eyes, Bigger is not only guilty of kidnapping Mary but of being a Communist and black. Significantly, they are all crimes for the investigator. Eventually, Mr. Dalton intervenes when he begins to believe Bigger's claims that the Communist pamphlets Bigger himself had planted in the drawer were given to him by Jan as part of a ploy to recruit him. The day before, Mary had asked Bigger about unions in front of her father. Mr. Dalton ends the questioning, convinced of Bigger's innocence, and unwilling to see him tortured further.

As Bigger leaves for his room, he hears Mr. Dalton and Britten talking Mr. Dalton tries to convince Britten that Bigger is troubled, but not truly bad. Britten is unresponsive; he says, "To me, a nigger's a nigger." The two men begin to talk about Jan as a suspect, although Mr. Dalton finds it uncharacteristic for Mary to go without telling anyone. The two men leave and Bigger retires to his room to strategize.

Unsettled, Bigger determines never to be caught off guard again and reviews his story in his head, hoping that Jan will lie to protect Mary, thereby implicating himself. Bigger also wants to face and better Britten, although he already feels equal to the white men because he killed Mary, a symbol of wealth and purity. Eventually, he sleeps, exhausted from being constantly alert. He dreams of carrying a head down a city street, only it is his own head. As he walks, he hears a bell tolling and knows that he will soon be found out. Though he tries to escape, he is surrounded. As a final attempt at freedom, he throws his head at the crowd. Clearly, Bigger sees himself as being thrown to the masses and knows that none of his attempts will stop the inevitable taking of his life. The head itself, symbolizing the place of racism and the site of Bigger's plotting and fear, becomes a metaphor for his struggle against white America. Bigger wakens to a real bell calling for him and the arrival of Jan, Britten and Mr. Dalton in his room.

The men gather and the questioning of Bigger and Jan begins. Bigger tells his lie, stating that Jan was at the house the night before. He feels enraged when Jan stares at him— enraged because he is hurting him, enraged because he feels guilt. Jan asks Bigger why he is lying, and who is putting him up to it. Bigger stares at the floor and refuses to answer, using the stereotype of the reluctant black servant to his advantage. When they ask if Jan saw Mary the night before, he lies, then recants, but the initial lie is enough to make him guilty in the eyes of Britten. Jan's responses work right into Bigger's plan. As the questioning continues, Jan is stunned to learn that Mary did not make it to Detroit, and he continues his entreaty for Bigger to tell the truth. As the interview closes, Mr. Dalton, overcome with worry for his daughter, begs Jan to bring her back. Then he offers him money. Insulted, Jan gives one last look at the three men, and storms out of the room. When Bigger looks up, Mr. Dalton is examining him. He asks if Bigger is telling the truth. Bigger tells him yes, and the two men leave, with Britten convinced that Jan is to blame.

Bigger leaves the house, eager to get away. He sees Jan at a corner store and tries to avoid him but Jan is determined to talk to Bigger, wanting to know why Bigger lied. Bigger keeps his hand on his gun, feeling the rage and fear well up inside him; he thinks if Jan doesn't leave him alone, he'll shoot. Jan asks Bigger to come for a cup of coffee then moves to grab his arm; Bigger pulls the gun and Jan backs away as Bigger screams to be left alone. Jan runs away, and Bigger buries the gun back in his shirt then walks to a drug store to buy ransom note materials. All around Bigger, falling snow blankets the city in white. Wright uses the snow as a metaphor for the white world and the way in which it surrounds Bigger and slows his progress, both literally and figuratively. Bigger looks at the city around him and sees the sign for the Dalton's real estate company, making vague sense of the Daltons' hypocrisy. They give millions to "Negro education" but they charge Bigger's family eight dollars a week for a rat-infested, one-room apartment. He believes the ransom note will 'jar them out of their senses.' He makes his way to Bessie's to prep her for the ransom drop.

When he arrives, she is sleepy and drunk and his faith in her wavers. They argue about the job until Bigger tells her that if she doesn't shut up and sit on the bed, he'll slap her. He sits down and begins the ransom letter, carefully plotting it to suggest that Mary is alive and that the culprit is a Communist. Bessie keeps asking if he is really going to do it. She begins to ask about Mary, convinced that Bigger has killed her. Eventually, he tells her, sealing her fate. Now that she knows the truth, Bessie can neither be trusted nor left alone. She begins sobbing; Bigger tries to feed her more alcohol until she reaches for the bottle herself then he withdraws it. She appeals to the Lord, begging for salvation, and Bigger tells her not to bother. The two continue arguing until he threatens her with a knife. He then takes her out to show her the drop spot— a large white abandoned building. He enters and checks the place over with his flashlight. When he notices Bessie missing, he finds her sobbing outside. He smacks her across the face and threatens to do more if she doesn't pull herself together, then he reviews the plan with her. Bessie finally agrees to do it, claiming she was already lost the moment she got together with Bigger. She sees that her life is over, either from his violence or from getting caught. She knows her fate.

Bigger leaves her and returns to the Dalton's where he slips the ransom note under the door of the house and enters the basement. He stands in front of the furnace, wanting to shift the coals to see if Mary burned completely, but he can't bring himself to do it. Instead, he goes to bed tired and hungry, and has a panic attack. Unnerved, he heads down to the kitchen where Peggy has left plates of food. When Peggy turns the corner, he sees that she has the note in her hand and excitement overwhelms him. Though he feels unable, he forces himself to eat, to look normal. Peggy returns and begins to make idle conversation about the fears Mary's disappearance awakened. Bigger listens, trying to eat faster and leave the kitchen. As she talks, he thinks about how the family will respond to the note, how they will assume that a white man did it, because a black man would not have sufficient intelligence and guts to plan such a thing. Suddenly, Mr. Dalton bursts into the kitchen with the open letter in his hand. He asks Peggy where and when she got it. Mrs. Dalton enters, senses her husband's tension, and asks what happened. He doesn't answer, but asks who left the letter. Both Peggy and Bigger claim ignorance, and Mr. Dalton finally reveals the contents of the note: Mary has been kidnapped. Mrs. Dalton begins to sob, and Peggy prays that Mary is alive. Mrs. Dalton faints, and Mr. Dalton picks her up and walks through the door Bigger holds for them. Left alone, Bigger follows the Daltons, trying to eavesdrop. He hears Dalton ask for Britten. Bigger escapes to his room.

From his room, he hears Peggy crying and opening the door for Britten, who asks her a series of questions about Bigger. Peggy answers that Bigger is "just a quiet colored boy … He's just like all the other colored boys." Again, racist assumptions work to Bigger's advantage; he is imagined too stupid to do anything, although Britten is suspicious and continues asking whether Bigger appears comfortable with white people and whether he talks with his hands as if he has been around Jews. Britten associates Communism with Jewish people, and he has a prejudice against both. As Bigger listens, Britten stops the questioning and is joined by other male voices. They talk about whether or not Dalton should call the police. Dalton, to protect Mary, decides to follow the ransom note. Britten says he will wait for the signal. Bigger begins to worry about what will happen when Jan gets picked up by the police. He hopes that by signing Red to the ransom note that the police will continue to look for Communists. Like his mother and sister, Bigger has no real desire to be seen or examined closely. He wants to be as non-descript as possible. He expends a great deal of effort on misdirection. A little while later, Britten continues his interrogation of Bigger, eager to get Bigger to name Jan as the killer. Bigger crafts his answers, using all of the Communist and racial stereotypes he knows. He talks about the Communist quest for equality, knowing that the very concept will enrage and terrify Britten. He hopes that this tide of emotion will carry Britten away from Bigger as a suspect.

As the two men talk, men from the press arrive. They enter the house against Britten's will, eager to get the story. They bring with them newspapers full of news about Jan's arrest. Bigger knows the media control the case on many levels. The press suggest the killer and what should be done to him. They dictate his actions, help him to make his plans. As they file into the basement, Bigger perceives them as harder than Britten and less austere than Mr. Dalton. They mill around like dogs, eager to pounce on the scoop. One slips Bigger money to tell him the inside story. Bigger returns the money. Britten tells the newsmen that Mr. Dalton will not see them until Tuesday; Bigger tries to move despite his lack of sleep. The newsmen bristle at the news and bombard Britten with questions about Mary's whereabouts, Jan's accusation that Mr. Dalton is trying to slander the Party and destroy his relationship with Mary, and Jan's comments about Bigger being paid to lie about Jan. Britten tries to field the questions, but Mr. Dalton steps in, defending Bigger. Dalton asks for silence, and the men comply. Behind him, Mrs. Dalton opens the door. She is an almost theatrical white figure who captures the attention of all the men present. The Daltons touch hands, and Mr. Dalton announces

Jan's release, his own apology for the arrest and the fact that Mary has been kidnapped. The press leaps, asking why she was kidnapped, who might have done it—all that they know. They ask, to take pictures of the ransom note and Dalton refuses, shielding it from the press. They ask finally, how it is signed. Dalton tells them: 'Red'. He adds that it is followed by the hammer and sickle symbol of the Party. Bigger watches as the press photograph the Daltons, giving the couple blocking to make the picture more pathetic, then the couple leaves. After a few more questions, the men become silent. They then turn to Bigger. One of the men opens the furnace door and peeks inside. They ask to see Mary's room, leaving Bigger alone in the basement to investigate the newspaper.

The paper has typical digs at the Party and a picture of Mary, which morphs in Bigger's head to be Mary's severed head. After he reads the story, he drops the paper as the press returns to the basement. Bigger goes back to playing dumb, answering their questions because Britten told him to. Eventually, the press tires of Bigger and returns to Britten who urges them to give Dalton time to find his daughter before they ask too many questions. The men gather themselves to phone in their reports and Bigger realizes that he must clean the ashes out of the furnace soon. He wants to wait until the men are gone in case any of Mary's bones have failed to burn. Then, a reporter bursts back into the room with news; Jan will not leave jail. The press interepret this as proof positive of Jan's guilt, claiming that he doesn't want to lead the police to her hiding place. Further, Jan claims to have alibis who will swear to his presence the night of Mary's kidnapping. Britten turns to Bigger to confirm his earlier statement, which Bigger does although with increasing fear. The press turn to him again, questioning him. Flustered, Bigger tries to answer, playing as dumb as possible. The men tire of him and Peggy brings coffee to the men. Britten urges Bigger to reveal the night at the restaurant to the press, giving them reason to mistrust Jan and his Communist ways. They ask pointed questions, trying to get Bigger to reinforce the schism between whites and blacks, asking him if he felt uncomfortable, not 'right' eating with whites. The press sees a story; the

Communists force blacks to engage with them, although African Americans want whites and blacks to be separate as well. One even claims, "I'm slanting this to the primitive Negro who doesn't want to be disturbed by white civilization." In many ways, these claims reinforce the ideas propagated by movies like *Trader Horn* as well as those ideas put forth by the paper itself. They continue to ask if Jan is Jewish, hoping to get a second popular stigma against the Communist. With their angle firmly established, they photograph an unsuspecting Bigger. Peggy brings sugar and milk for the coffee and tells Bigger to clean out the furnace. Knowing that disobeying would seem odd, Bigger turns to the furnace and labors his tired brain for a solution. He tries to rake down the coals, but his efforts choke the fire and smoke pours into the basement. Men yell at him, telling him what to do as Bigger coughs, then one of the men grabs the shovel and begins to dig out the bin. Bigger considers running but thinks he still has a chance for the ransom money until one of the men begins to examine the ashes, finding bone and jewelry. As he calls his colleagues near, Bigger realizes he needs to escape and slips up the steps, locks the door behind him, and turns out the light. He jumps out the window, wetting himself in the process as he lands in a pile of snow. He escapes down side streets, knowing that self-preservation is the only remaining plan. He feels for his gun and thinks that he will shoot before he lets the police take him. He knows that for a black man accused of killing a white woman, death is the result either way.

He makes his way back to the South Side, pausing to read the paper. In the current issue, Jan is still the object of suspicion which buys Bigger a little time. Bigger knows that the Daltons and the picture taken of them will stir great sympathy, and make the world hate not only Bigger but all black men. Any man who looks like Bigger will be under suspicion. All black men will be on trial. He finds Bessie and tells her Mary has been found. Bessie sobs, knowing that she too will be discovered. Bigger threatens to leave if Bessie doesn't stop. She stops crying and asks what happened. For the first time, Bigger tells the story, revealing its accidental nature. Immediately,

Bessie sees the conclusions the white world will draw; Bigger will be marked a rapist, then killed. Bigger thinks,

> Yes, he had raped her. Every time he felt as he had felt that night, he raped. But rape was not what one did to women. Rape was what one felt when one's back was against a wall and one had to strike out, whether one wanted to or not, to keep the pack from killing one. He committed rape every time he looked into a white face. He was a long, taut piece of rubber, which a thousand white hands had stretched to the snapping point, and when he snapped it was rape. But it was rape when he cried out in hate deep in his heart as he felt the strain of living day by day. That, too, was rape (228).

Wright's presentation of Bigger's interior monologue predates much of modern conversation about rape and its origins in power struggle. Rape is not about desire, it is about exerting power and control. Bigger finally exerts his own power through violence and hatred, committing rape, which becomes killing Mary, and beating up Gus. He transfers his position from victim to victimizer without ever really rescinding his position as victim. He is simultaneously both when he kills Mary and attacks Gus.

Bigger and Bessie prepare to leave, the former utterly exhausted. They gather bedding and liquor and head for the abandoned buildings they had scouted. Bessie wails that Bigger has used her and caused her nothing but trouble, "just plain black trouble." Here, the term black refers not only to color but the circumstance. As she talks, Bigger determines that Bessie can neither be left behind nor brought along. They go to the building and set up the bedding. The two lay down and Bigger rapes Bessie. After he finishes, Bessie falls asleep and Bigger finds two bricks and beats her head in. He figures that for him to survive, it must be her life for his. He imagines in his head a "white blur hovering near, of Mary burning, of Britten, of the law tracking him down." Though he initially panics at of the thought of killing Bessie, being hunted makes Bigger numb and he smashes the brick into her head. He takes her body and throws it out a window, tossing the blood soaked bedding on top of her. He remembers the money from Mary's purse is in Bessie's pocket. Bigger refuses to go collect it, believing that if he sees the body again the guilt will overwhelm him. Instead, he tries to sleep but his mind continues to race. He thinks

And, yet, out of it all, over and above all that had happened, impalpable but real, there remained to him a queer sense of power. *He* had done this. *He* had brought all this about. In all of his life these two murders were the most meaningful things that had ever happened to him. He was living, truly and deeply, no matter what others might think, looking at him with their blind eyes. Never had he had the chance to live out the consequences of his actions; never had his will been so free as in this night and day of fear and murder and flight (239).

Bigger finally has what the white population has had for years. The opportunity to make real choices with real consequences. Finally in command of his fate, for better or for worse, he has the sense of living autonomously, although his choices have resulted in dire consequences. He is no longer a blind man being led through the narrow maze of preordained options dictated by the white community. Further, Wright explains the schism in Bigger's intellectual and emotional life:

There was something he *knew* and something he *felt*; something the *world* gave him and something he *himself* had; something spread out in *front* of him and something spread out in *back*; and never in all his life, with this black skin of his, had the two worlds, thought and feeling, will and mind, aspiration and satisfaction, been together; never had he felt a sense of wholeness.

In his alienation, Bigger lacks the ability to trust his own impressions and intuition. He has never been taught to connect intellect and feeling. All of his impulses have been so long suppressed that he is no longer capable of understanding something fully; he can only react. He thinks of his mother and Bessie, critiques the ways in which they handle their oppression. His mother escapes in religion; Bessie escapes in alcohol. Both give their autonomy over for temporary comfort. Bigger rejects both. As he thinks, the sun rises and a sleepless Bigger is forced to continue his hiding in the white blanketed Chicago. Wright uses the snowstorm, and its all encompassing nature, to represent the white world and Bigger's travails through it. It impedes and hides him simultaneously.

Bigger heads to the street, searching for the newspaper to keep him abreast of his own case. The headline reads, "Hunt Black in Girl's Death." Bigger steals the paper and reads the accusations against him, "Authorities hint sex crime." Bigger sees it as a death sentence. The police force, five thousand strong combined with three thousand volunteers, have gone to the "Black Belt," searching every house and abandoned building and cutting off all exit roads. Continually, the papers refer to Bigger as "the Negro rapist and murderer." Around the city, blacks are losing the jobs as a result of white fear. The paper also notes two important things: first, the police still believe Jan to be involved, and second, a graph reveals the places where the authorities have already searched, showing Bigger how trapped he is. Bigger looks for an empty apartment; the paper had not mentioned them. He crouches in the snow, hiding and thinking, then looks out into the windows of an apartment in the projects. He sees a couple having sex with their three children watching—five people in a one-room apartment, without any privacy. He sees an empty building across the street that the city refuses to do anything with. All around him, hypocrisy winks. In the Black Belt, bread is one cent more than in the white section, rents are double for less space, the same jobs pay less money, and the majority of the black population is stuffed into the same small area. Though hungry, Bigger waits to find a black bakery, instead of the white bakeries, though he knows that the majority of the businesses in the Black Belt are owned by whites—another way in which blacks are stymied. Black funeral parlors exist only because whites do not want to touch black bodies.

Eventually, Bigger buys a loaf of bread and breaks into an empty flat where he overhears two black men talking. One claims that Bigger should have stayed and faced the authorities if he was guilty. Further, he believes that by running, Bigger has made every black man look guilty, which for this man resulted in a lost job. He thinks the white man can't be fought without losing everything. The other man believes that guilty or not, Bigger would be assumed a murderer simply because of his race and he stands in solidarity. Bigger tires of listening to them, eats his bread, and sleeps only to be woken by the Church music next door. He feels like the music is trying to lull him into giving himself up, with its claims that the next life will be better, that he should just surrender to God's will. Bigger leaves to gather another *Times*, to see where his case stands. He buys the paper and escapes to another empty apartment. He reads "24-Hour Search Fails to Unearth Rapist, Raid 1,000 Negro Homes, Incipient Riot Quelled at 47th and Halsted." The paper also showed another map of the search's progress. The apartment sits in the middle of the remaining white spot. Bigger plans to hide on the roof of the building until the hunting party passes; however, as he heads for the attic, he hears sirens. The police descend. Bigger looks out over the roofs and plans to run across them. If he cannot escape, he decides that he will jump and keep the police from getting him. All around, he hears the sounds of sirens and police, and below that, the screams and yells of terrified people whose homes the police have stormed. He sees a man pop his head into the roof space, then go down. He hears two men below him, talking about the sexual merit of a black woman in the household and bemoaning their exhaustion. They agree to look on the roof and as the first man pops his head up, Bigger, panic stricken, smashes his head with his gun. The man collapses in the snow, but his partner comes to find out what happened. Bigger tries to leave the roof and climbs on to a chimney to avoid being seen. As he debates options, more men pour onto the roof, answering the partner's call for help. The police surround the block and Bigger begins to move from icy ledge to icy ledge until, suddenly, someone spies him and shoots. Bigger runs across the roofs, stopping at a ledge, past which he cannot go. He considers shooting but knows that there will be more men than he has bullets and he cannot spare the time. He climbs the water tower in front of him, the white snow everywhere a visual reminder of the white world that hems him in. From there, he shoots at the approaching men. They throw tear gas onto the tower and Bigger knocks it off. Then they tell him to come down. Bigger vows to use all but one of his bullets on them and the last on himself. They will not take him alive.

The police call again, telling him that this is his last chance, then the fire department sprays the hose on him. Bigger begins to shake from cold, and they continue to call for his gun. He tries to reach for the gun but his fingers are frozen. The stream of water knocks Bigger off the tower. The men grab him and carry him down from the roof. They drag him down the stairs by his feet, letting his head bang on every step. At the bottom of the stairs, a crowd of white faces yell out for his death, "Lynch 'im!" and "Kill that black ape!" He lies in the snow, his arms outstretched and the men's boots on his ankles as if he is crucified. Then, he sinks into unconsciousness.

III. Fate

When the final section opens, Bigger exists in a kind of torpor. He does not eat, sleep, or respond to the stimulus around him. He feels neither fear nor hatred, no connection with his fellow humankind. Wright writes:

> Having been thrown by an accidental murder into a position where he sensed a possible order and meaning in his relations with the people about him; having accepted the moral guilt and responsibility for that murder because it made him feel free for the first time in his life; having felt in his heart some obscure need to be at home with people and having demanded ransom money to enable him to do it—having done all of this and failed, he chose not to struggle anymore (274).

When Bigger later talks with his attorney, this idea of purpose, freedom, and awareness comes back, and with it, an understanding of why he killed. Before the trial, the condition continues until the inquest where he is thrust into a crowd of white people who not only hate him—a feeling to which he is accustomed—but revile him and display an absolute certainty that he is both a killer and a rapist. The palpable blame snaps Bigger to attention and he notices that two of his fingernails are missing. He doesn't bother to imagine what might have happened to them. In this moment, Wright, who received criticism about creating hatred against whites, might have pressed his advantage here and added white on black police brutality to the story. However, he remains true to his character's blurred memory and continues with the present rather than the past. Bigger realizes not only that he is in physical pain, but he also notes the presence of the Daltons at the trial. Overcome with his state, he faints and awakens on a cot in a separate room. A policeman drops off a plate of food, which Bigger finds suddenly delicious. All the joys of being alive strike him in this moment—the taste of food, the automatic functioning of the salivary glands, all the things which make him alive.

After eating, Bigger asks for a newspaper, a way to re-enter the present. He finds himself the center of the news and deemed the "Negro sex-slayer." In nearly all references to Bigger, his race is stressed. The papers continually compare Bigger to an ape or an animal. They even suggest that his "criminal and intractable nature" stems from having a small portion of white in his blood, reiterating fears about the mating of whites and blacks. The *Jackson Daily Star* weighs in with the belief that citizens ought to take the law into their own hands as they allegedly do in the South, making "an example out of a trouble-making nigger." The paper's editor, reporting on Bigger's childhood, suggests that segregation and conditioning are the only ways to keep whites safe from blacks. Wright used the Robert Nixon murder case as fodder for a plotline he already knew well. The media's influence could not be underestimated in creating public outcry, heightening mob mentality/rage, and urging vigilante justice. With the media's spin, any verdict less than death would create a public furor. Wright's lengthy newspaper stories show the ways in which the media made public opinion, a prescient point.

Bigger finally lowers the paper, enraged that he has to be made the object of mockery before he dies. Even the act of murder, his only true act of free will, is made an object of ridicule. Bigger considers trying to escape back into his torpor but it is not possible. Instead, he lets himself drift to sleep. He is awakened by his mother's preacher, Reverend Hammond. Hammond kneels in front of Bigger and begins praying. Bigger tries to block it out, associating the sound with his mother and childhood and with the fact that even with God he would be found guilty. The preacher urges Bigger to forget the papers and to forget that he is black. The preacher claims that God does not see skin color, implying that even the preacher has subconsciously absorbed the racist attitudes surrounding him. Bigger drifts, remembering the visions the Church had promised him as a child. When he resurfaces, he feels more guilt for having given up those dreams than for killing Mary. He believes that ridding himself of the vision of a better life was his first murder, the one that began all those that would follow. He thinks that to live his life, to withstand it, he "had created a new world for himself, and for that he was to die." The preacher continues, asking Bigger to open his heart to God and giving him a crucifix. Reverend Hammond tells Bigger the cross is the world and the suffering man nailed to it is life. Hammond stops talking suddenly as Jan enters the cell.

Bigger sits terrified on his cot uncertain as to why Jan is there. Jan begins to speak, and Bigger realizes for the first time that Jan is not angry; instead, he apologizes to Bigger, claiming that he did not realize his own ignorance when he first spoke with Bigger and forced him to socialize with him and Mary. Jan understands the limits of Bigger's life and his choices. He offers him friendship, which confuses Bigger. The Reverend begins speaking with Jan, who claims to have gained something from the experience surrounding Mary's murder. Like Bigger, his blindness has ended. He sees into the hearts of men, he better understands what motivates them. To illustrate his new understanding and his desire to befriend Bigger in a meaningful way, he offers the services of his friend, Jewish lawyer Boris A. Max, from the Labor Defenders. Bigger feels guilty for his treatment of Jan in the face of Jan's newfound belief in Bigger and the necessity of his crime. This is also the first time that Bigger sees a white person as a human being, as someone who he has hurt. Again, the metaphor of blindness returns—Bigger's realization allows him to see Jan for the first time.

Jan's offer unsettles the reverend, who is reluctant to bring Communism into an already inflamed situation and worried that the connection will further incite the angry, racist mobs. In this moment, Wright shows two major ideologies doing battle: Jan believes that the newspapers incite rage, violence and racial attitudes and that only education and public battles can change those attitudes. The Reverend believes that only God can erase the hatred, a somewhat less pro-active approach. Bigger urges Jan to forget him, but Jan presses his point, saying, "You believed enough to kill. You thought you were settling something, or you wouldn't have killed." His observation renders Bigger speechless, and Jan ushers Max into the room. Max asks if Bigger will allow them to represent him; Bigger repeats that he has no money, reinforcing the fact that low-income people are significantly less likely to get legal representation than upper class people. Max takes the case and offers Bigger some cigarettes as Buckley, the state's attorney, enters the room. The hostility between the two men is clear, as are Buckley's political predispositions. He says, "What in hell you Reds get out of bothering with a black thing like that, God only knows,..." Max reveals that part of his intention in defending Bigger is to defend the Communist Party against the slurs perpetrated by the state in the newspapers and his belief that men like Buckley created Bigger and others like him. He seeks to explain the circumstances that led Bigger to act as he did. Buckley continues to try to get Bigger to speak, telling him that the gathered evidence has already convicted him. Bigger feels whatever confidence Jan and Max had given him dissolve. Buckley powerplays Max, asking the Daltons to enter the room.

Mr. Dalton asks the lawyers if Bigger has confessed who helped him do the job; they are still convinced that the scope of the crime requires a white brain. The Reverend offers his apologies to the Daltons, making special note of their "good work." The Daltons explain that they wanted to help Bigger, educate him; a confused Mr. Dalton even notes that just that day he had sent twelve ping-pong tables to the South Side Boys' Club. Max jumps in, articulating much of what Wright himself learned while working in Chicago:

> "Will ping-pong keep men from murdering? Can't you *see*? Even after losing your daughter, you're going to keep going in the same direction? Don't you grant as much life-feeling to other men as you have? Could *ping-pong* have kept you from making your millions? This boy and millions like him want a meaningful life, not ping-pong… (295)"

Mr. Dalton responds typically, saying he did not cause the state of affairs, nor can he, as one man, change them. Max begins to argue but at this point, Bigger's family arrives. Many critics attack this portion of the narrative, claiming the incredulity of having this many people in the same cell at the same time. Wright defends himself as a novelist. He used poetic license because the scene creates the effect he is looking for, pitting ideologies against each other in a small jail cell.

Bigger is ashamed to have his family there, to have them see him and to have others see them. His mother, in hysterics, runs and hugs him. He looks past her to see his siblings and friends. Intensely aware of the white gaze, Bigger feels ashamed, then decides that none of them should be ashamed, "Had he not taken fully upon himself the crime of being black? Had he not done the thing which they dreaded above all others? Then they ought not stand here, and pity him, cry over him; but look at him and go home, contented, feeling that their shame was washed away." His brother Buddy walks over to him and says, "Listen, Bigger, if you didn't do it, just tell me and I'll fix 'em. I'll get a gun and fill four or five of 'em…." The white people gasp and his mother begs him to stop; Buddy remains unmoved, emboldened by his brother's actions. Bigger, wanting to reassure his family and defy the white people around him, tells his mother not to worry and that he will be out soon. The room silences and his mother asks if there is anything that she can do. The question is absurd; they are poor blacks living off of the public welfare system. Bigger regrets his words, hoping they are not the words by which his family remembers him. He acknowledges the lie by telling her nothing can be done. He wants them to leave. Wright narrates Bigger's subconscious understanding: he distanced himself from them so that he would not feel the shame, despair, and hate that overwhelm him now. One by one, the rest of his friends and family speak to him, and he realizes that he was not alone in his life or his actions; they were intertwined with his family and friends. His mother suggests that he turn himself over to God. He urges her over and over to forget him. He tells her that he will pray, believing it to be a lie. Then he hugs his family members as the Reverend chants a prayer.

Before leaving, Mrs. Thomas appeals to Mrs. Dalton, as a mother, not to let Bigger be killed. The men race to separate the women. Mrs. Dalton tells her she can do nothing; all she could have done was try to educate Bigger. Her blindness becomes more than physical. Mrs. Thomas articulates the difference in their positions: the Daltons are rich and powerful, the Thomases have nothing. The Daltons will not be swayed, though they are not unsympathetic. Mrs. Dalton tells her to concentrate on her other two children; Mr. Dalton tells her that he will save her from having to move. She thanks them, sobbing; as Bigger watches her, his shame at her outburst turns to hate. Everyone leaves save Buckley, who takes Bigger to the window to listen to and see the mob screaming for his blood. Then, he urges Bigger to confess.

He tells Bigger that his resistance is pointless, and tries to get Bigger to implicate Jan. When Bigger stays silent, Buckley tells him that Bessie was found alive, but died of exposure. He also tries to pin two additional murders and sexual assaults on Bigger, which the latter vehemently denies. But, having broken Bigger's silence, Buckley pushes harder, asking if Jan and Bigger had tag team relations with Mary. He reveals his knowledge of the foiled Blum plot, making Bigger believe that Buckley knows nearly everything that happened, except for his insistence on Bigger's involvement with Jan and the other murders. Buckley focuses particularly on the ransom note, convinced that the intricacy of the crime required two things: premeditation and the intellect of a white man. In both cases, he is wrong, but his line of questioning reveals the certainty with which Buckley, and others like him, regard the minds of black people as inept and unintelligent. Bigger wants to tell Buckley what happened, but he believes that he can never articulate what he sees as the vital part of the crime: the motive. Wright writes: "He would have gladly admitted his guilt had he thought that in doing so he could have also given in the same breath a sense of the deep, choking hate that had been his life, a hate that he had not wanted to have, but could not help having (308)."

Buckley, unaware of Bigger's impulse to tell, claims that he can make Bigger a deal—in exchange for a confession he will have Bigger sent to a mental hospital rather than to death. He resists, not wanting to be called crazy. His motives did not stem from insanity; they grew from circumstance. Buckley, sure of his control of the situation, calls in the stenographer and Bigger gives a full confession. With the confession gathered, Buckley gives up all pretense of sympathy, looking at Bigger and saying, "Just a scared colored boy from Mississippi." He leaves and Bigger slides to the floor and sobs, "wondering what it was that had hold of him, why he was here." He fears trusting his feelings as Jan and Max told him. The feelings betrayed him when he confessed, as he was unable to fully articulate why he had killed. They betrayed him with the crimes he committed. He feels lost as to what to do.

Before he can think deeply, he is returned to the inquest where an angry crowd greets him with a roar and a physical rush forward which policemen restrain. The trial begins with Mrs. Dalton called to the stand to give family background. Bigger sees around him the accoutrements of his crime and the pale visage of Mrs. Dalton, a sure pathos builder by the prosecution. Buckley places the twisted remains of a family heirloom (an earring) into Mrs. Dalton's hand. She identifies it and tells the events of the night of Mary's death. During the questioning, Buckley makes sure to insinuate rape, asking Mrs. Dalton if she felt able to detect whether her daughter had been sexually assaulted. Though the mother says that she did not think she could, the suggestion settles in the minds of the already enraged crowd. Buckley continues with his theatrical style, asking the jury to view the remains of Mary Dalton, a pile of white bones on a table. Then Buckley calls Jan, and Bigger wonders if he can trust any white man, even this one who offered him friendship.

Buckley composes a series of yes or no questions which incriminate Jan by omission. He begins by establishing Jan as a Communist and a man who wants equality between whites and blacks. He will later use this suggest that Jan delivered a drunk, sexually vulnerable Mary to Bigger. He refers to her as "bait." Max turns to the coroner to decry the validity of the questions asked, claiming they inflame the public and have no relation to the case. He is quickly silenced, and Buckley continues to ask questions that portray Jan as a "Negro lover" and Communist, the two being unforgiveable sins in the eyes of the public. Again, Max objects and is overruled. The court becomes a place to make an example of both Communists and African Americans as evils to be destroyed and oppressed. At the end of the questioning, Jan is visibly frustrated and upset, and Bigger begins to understand that he is not the only person on trial.

Buckley then calls Mr. Dalton to the stand. Dalton explains the ways in which he and his family tried to help the "Negro boys" they hired, how he had tried to protect Bigger, and how shocked he was when Bigger appeared guilty. When Buckley finishes, Max begins to question Dalton, establishing the fact that Dalton owns the stock of the company that owns the slum in which the Thomases live. Max dismantles attempts by Dalton to distance himself from the money trail and his questioning incites the coroner who demands that Max stop harassing Dalton. Max claims the same latitude allowed in earlier questioning and asserts that he too is establishing Bigger's influences. Mr. Dalton agrees with Max, asking that he continue despite the court's bias. Interestingly, Wright is very light-handed with Dalton, making him both a part of an abberant system as well as a sympathetic character contrary to charges by some critics that the book blindly spurs hatred against whites. Max, Jan and Dalton are in direct opposition to that claim.

Max makes his attack, demanding to know why Dalton charges higher rates to blacks for tiny apartments in gross disrepair. He demands to know why Dalton will not rent to African Americans anywhere else in the city and why it is that he assumes that black people want to live in a clump on the South Side. He continues asking Dalton why he doesn't use the millions he gives to charitable donations to lower the rent for his tenants. Dalton claims that to do so would be illegally underselling his competitors. Max then asks Dalton why he contributes money to African American causes and whether Dalton has ever employed one of the black men that he has educated. For the former, he has no answer, for the latter, he admits that he has never hired any of the men he paid to educate. With this damning questioning complete, Max rests. He then tells the court that Bigger will not be testifying, and Buckley tells the jury to look at the evidence and the weapons used in the crime. Then he reveals a last trick.

Two men wheel in Bessie's dead body for jury examination. Max objects, claiming the body is meant only to incite violence; the state's attorney claims it is valuable evidence regarding the nature of the crimes committed. Wright describes the shock in the courtroom; Bessie's death had been withheld until this moment. Her body was not presented as a crime but as evidence of his guilt in killing Mary. The white girl's body would never have been wheeled into the courtroom and made into evidence and spectacle. As Bigger rightly notes, he is not particularly on trial for killing Bessie, he is on trial for killing a white woman. The court's use of Bessie suggests that it is more than hatred of whites that spurred his desire to kill, that if he will kill both within and without his race, then he is a monster without bounds and as such, he should be killed. Bigger feels enraged that he lived as whites told him to and where they told him to. When he finally broke free by killing, he is back under their control because of his punishment. He is not simply a man on trial, but is a *black* man on trial. The men finally wheel Bessie's covered body away, and Bigger tries not to black out. The jury urges a trial and that Bigger be held until said trial. Max tells him that he will be back to see him that night.

Two policeman escort Bigger out the front door of the courthouse where a mob awaits, ready to perpetrate vigilante justice. Bigger is put in a police car and driven to the Dalton's where he is ordered to repeat the events of the murder night. He refuses, telling them that they can only make him die now, nothing else. Eventually, the officers give up and walk him through a crowd of people who spit on him and try to attack him. When he looks up, he sees a burning cross atop a building across the street. Though Bigger does not know what it is, the reader recognizes the symbol of the Ku Klux Klan. He is thrust in a car and brought to jail. Bigger compares the burning cross to the cross of Jesus, fear versus love, panic versus calm; he remembers what the burning cross means and in his rage he rips the cross from around his neck. The policemen tell him to keep it and insist that only God can help him, but Bigger feels abandoned by religion and refuses both the cross and the preacher come to see him. The preacher picks up the cross, and Bigger tells him not to come closer. But the guard opens the door, and just as the preacher steps in, Bigger slams it in his face, sending him sprawling. The preacher leaves and Bigger resigns himself to being without the hope of religion.

Bigger awakens the next day to find a newspaper sent by Max which outlined Bigger's guilt as a rapist and murderer as well as Buckley's assertion that he was in collusion with the Communists. The article ends with Buckley joking with the press about his upcoming re-election plans. Bigger's reading is interrupted when a hysterical black man is thrust into his cell, screaming for the return of papers. Other inmates tell Bigger that the man was doing research on the lives of colored people and that he went crazy. The man himself claims that his professor called the police and had him sent away. His crazed behavior distracts and terrifies Bigger and causes a din to rise among the other inmates. In the midst of it, Bigger is pulled away to see Max.

Max offers Bigger some clothes and asks after his welfare. Bigger tells him not to bother with him and that nothing can be done. Max urges him to fight, to believe in himself, to fight for all of the other men who might be pushed around after an example is made of Bigger. Max continues to talk with Bigger, asking about the details of the night and Bigger's thoughts on it. Bigger explains that he hated Mary and that he may have wanted to rape her but didn't, though his skin color will find him guilty of rape in court. He tells the story, trying to figure out exactly what it was he was feeling. He hates Mary for crossing the line and extending the invitation to be equal, which Bigger knew would be rescinded. He wanted to rape her to exercise power over her, to show the people who say that black men are violent that he will fulfill the prophecy they made with a greater ferocity than they could have imagined, and yet, her death is also an accident. His fear of consequences led him to kill her. He explains that he hated her before he met her because white people had kept him and all other black men and women from succeeding and doing meaningful things. Max asks him what he wanted to do that was denied him, and Bigger can barely answer; he says that he knew nothing would be possible, so he never dreamed of anything. At every turn, the facts of racial prejudice account for much of Bigger's responses and behaviors.

Max continues the conversation, asking, finally, why Bigger killed the women. Bigger admits that he feels nothing for the dead women. Instead, he felt free after Mary's murder. He wasn't scared because he had already done the worst thing that he could imagine. He no longer had to worry about what he might do, it was already done. For that moment, he was outside of white law. Bigger talks about never feeling at home and always worrying about money. He talks about what he could not do, about wanting to do something that had meaning. Max asks if the boys club helped, and Bigger claims it only provided a place to plan their petty robberies. Wright used his knowledge from working at a boy's club to write the scene. Bigger then claims that religion gives nothing to people either, despite his mother's fervor. He states that he wanted to be happy in this world, not the next, and that religion, in addition to being useless, seemed a way of keeping black people from rebelling. He tells Max that black politicians are as bad as white. They too look down on the poor people of their race and, quite literally, buy their votes. Bigger also reveals that he felt the violence in him was inevitable and that Max is going to be hated for helping him. Still, Max brings Bigger a small amount of comfort because he does not judge and he listens to what Bigger had to say. He also tells Bigger that he will try to get the judge and the people to understand Bigger's life and motivations.

Bigger has a small moment of transformation after they talk. For the first time, someone really listened to what he had to say, and Bigger finds himself feeling more relaxed then he has ever felt in his life. The chance to articulate his world gives him momentary peace and a glimpse at the white world as being more than a monolith. He can separate the white hate into individual people, like Max and Jan and even Buckley. They begin to differentiate in a way that the white mob will never differentiate the black community. His mind resists the thought, worried that it will cause hope then disappointment, then breakdown.

In the cell, he spins through thoughts about equality and death. He wonders if there is something common between men, if they might be brought together, and the thought so intrigues him that it nearly keeps him from wanting death. Instead, he wants answers and the thought of dying before he understands brings him to sobs.

The trial is set for the next week. Bigger has entered a plea of not guilty, which Max plans to change when the trial begins. Bigger wants to again feel the hope and faith that Max had inspired in him. He worries that without it he will have no emotional resources with which to face the hatred of the white mob. He wants to feel certain of something, the goodness of man, the justice of God, the motive behind his actions; instead he feels adrift, unable to articulate or control his feelings. When his family comes to visit, he claims to be at peace but the lie enrages him because he wants so badly to be at peace. He reads newspaper accounts, sent over by the Communists, portraying him as living in luxury. He also reads that the city is in an uproar, with violence just beneath the surface. A psychiatrist attests to Bigger's sanity, and another claims that black men are unnaturally attracted to white women, compelled to have them. Max comes to bring him to trial and tells him that he may have to speak at the trial, but Bigger balks. Max tells him that the trial is larger than Bigger; he claims that every African American is on trial that day.

The trial recommences with the formal reading of Bigger's crimes. Max stuns the courtroom by pleading guilty on Bigger's behalf, claiming that his actions can be understood through an examination of the man's mental and emotional circumstances. Immediately, Buckley objects, claiming that Bigger cannot plead both insane and guilty. Max rejoins that he has no intention of claiming insanity, rather that Bigger is a product of his surroundings and the racial tensions in which he reached maturation and thereby less responsible for his crimes. Max is trying to prove degrees of sanity and degrees of blame based on societal pressure and attitudes. He contends that society created Bigger and must deal with the consequences by preventing the circumstances that lead him to commit crimes. After the lawyers finish arguing with each other, the judge asks Bigger to stand. Inside, he wants to react with violence, to do something to end the unfair advantage against him. Instead, he stands when Max urges. The judge asks Bigger a series of questions to make sure that he understands the consequences of pleading guilty, which may include lifetime imprisonment, death, or, at the very least, fourteen years imprisonment.

Buckley begins a histrionic opening statement done to incite the crowd both inside and outside of the courtroom. Though Max objects and the judge sustains his objection, Buckley continues his highly dramatic rendering of the case and Bigger's status as a monster, a black, sexually aggressive monster. As he progresses, he also argues against Max's conviction that society is part of the problem. Buckley claims if Bigger knows what a guilty plea is, then he knows the difference between right and wrong. He also implies that Max is trying to make Bigger appear insane, an implication to which Max objects. At the end of his soliliquoy, Buckley claims to have sixty witnesses; Max has significantly fewer as the case was raced to the top of the docket, which Max claims was done to appease the rage of the people. Max reiterates that he is going to prove that "his extreme youth, his mental and emotional life, and the reason he has pleaded guilty, should and must mitigate his punishment (376)."

Max continues his argument, claiming that Bigger will not be fairly tried because he is poor and black. He also asserts that the courts rushed the case due to popular feeling, which, in effect, leaves the state at the mercy of mob rule. He asks only that the court spare Bigger's life due to the facts of his upbringing. The court rests for an hour, then returns and Buckley parades his witnesses through the court to prove both Bigger's sanity, which is not actually in question, and his guilt. Newspapermen and teachers attest to his sanity, doctors to Bessie's rape, and waitresses to his presence in Ernie's Kitchen with Mary and Jan. By the end of the session, Bigger no longer cares who comes. He returns to his cell weary and Max tells him he must fight for his life.

When court contiues, Buckley brings in the theater manager to tell of Bigger's masturbating in the theater, a man from juvenile court talks about stolen tires, and a white woman, about Mary's size, crawls into a furnace to prove that she would fit. Eventually Buckley rests. The next morning, Bigger gets to the table before Max and feels terror without Max there to protect him. When Max arrives, he assures Bigger that he will do all he can. He launches into his defense, clarifying for the court that the decision is broader than the courtroom, indeed, he claims, it "touches the destiny of an entire nation (382)." He calls the death penalty the path of least resistance. He argues that the state must take responsibility for the circumstances that led to Bigger's crime: his poverty, his race. He notes that thousands of African-

American homes were searched and that African Americans were assaulted on the streets. He says,

> The hunt for Bigger Thomas served as an excuse to terrorize the entire Negro population, to arrest hundreds of Communists, to raid labor union headquarters and workers' organizations. Indeed, the tone of the press, the silence of the church, the attitude of the prosecution and the stimulated temper of the people are of such a nature as to indicate that *more* than revenge is being sought upon a man who has committed a crime (385).

He asserts that these groups have long been hated, that the current uproar is a result of political machinations. Buckley wants to get re-elected, so he pledged to stop relief demonstrations. In fact, he lists a series of government officials who support the rich, the businessmen of Chicago who are against labor unions and humane treatment of the poor. He claims that the public need to kill Bigger stems from fear and guilt, which led to hatred. That hatred stemmed from slavery and has grown from continued oppression. He also claims that the white hatred and fear is a counterpoint to Bigger's own hatred and fear.

He traces the hatred and fear back to slavery, to the ways in which African Americans created their own (centuries old) society out of necessity. Max says,

> ... injustice blots out one form of life, but another grows up in its place with its own rights, needs, and aspirations. What is happening here today is not injustice, but *oppression*, an attempt to throttle or stamp out a new form of life. It is this new form of life that has grown up here in our midst that puzzles us, that expresses itself, like a weed growing from under a stone, in terms we call crime. Unless we grasp this problem in the light of this new reality, we cannot do more than salve our feelings of guilt and rage with more murder when a man, living under such conditions, commits an act which we call a crime (391).

Max then claims that by killing Bigger all of the black men and women in America will feel more tightly bound by their social conditions, more enraged, more displaced, which will in turn perpetuate both the violence and the hatred. According to Max, the murderous intent already existed in Bigger; it was simply a matter of time before he had the opportunity to release it. He urges the court to stop believing that the specter of slavery, its repurcussions, and its oppressed people are dead. Shoving them into a tiny geographic space and bleeding their money away does not make them disappear, as killing Bigger will not do away with the larger social problems that created him and others like him.

Max then attacks each member of the Dalton family: Mary for her well-intentioned kindness that never understood the vast gulf between Bigger and herself, Mr. Dalton for keeping blacks in slums then offering them ping-pong tables or the occasional job, and Mrs. Dalton for her blind faith in an educational system that pays no attention to the black plight. He claims that Mary's death can mean something; she can become the reason that whites and blacks are no longer strangers. She can be the reason Chicago examines its oppression of African Americans. Max then cites education for creating in Bigger a desire to be something more and for creating in him the knowledge that to strive for it would be pointless. Echoing Wright, Max says that "religion, gambling and sex drain[ing] off their energies into channels harmful to them and profitable to us." Without that, he claims that more people would be on trial for violence. When Bigger brought Mary home drunk, he could not go to her parents because of the taboos and the distance created by racism. Max follows by saying that Bigger had no recourse for the wrongs done to him by society. His class and his race ensured that he would not receive equal treatment under the law just as it ensured he could not tell the Daltons that their daughter was drunk.

Max makes his most incredible statement to the court: that Bigger's killing Mary was the only thing in Bigger's life that had meaning. He later calls it an act of creation; Bigger chose to accept his crime, to try to make something from it, to choose the next step in his life. Nothing else had afforded him that opportunity. Max also reveals that Bigger felt no remorse for what he had done. The lawyer likens it to war—kill or be killed. He continues talking about the rights of man under the Constitution, making the famous claim that "men can starve from a lack of self-realization as much as they can from a lack of bread (399)!" He explains that Bigger's treatment and murder of Bessie was secondary to Mary's death, circumstantial insofar as Bigger killed her to keep from being killed by the white mob chasing him for Mary's death. He describes Bigger's relationship with Bessie; love was not an option in Bigger's life or Bessie's. Where and how could it grow?

He questions the mob outside as well, claiming a civil war might happen again if race relations continue in the same fashion. He asserts that to kill Bigger would be to again turn away from the truths about the lives of black people in America, to reinforce the status quo. He finishes with an impassioned plea to save not only Bigger's life but the morality of the public. Then he turns to Bigger, who is proud to be the center of so impassioned a speech. Max wearily says he did the best he could.

Bigger is returned to his cell, where he shares a smoke with Max. Back in court, Buckley delivers his own impassioned speech, attacking Max for invoking race and class though he himself uses racially loaded terms and stereotypes of black men hungry for white women. He says, "Every decent white man in America ought to swoon with joy for the opportunity to crush with his heel the woolly head of this black lizard, to keep him from scuttling on his belly farther over the earth and spitting forth his venom of death (409)." The comment makes the black man the equivalent of Satan and the white man the vengeful god. It also notes that black men should be contained. This kind of language and innuendo is typical of Buckley's remarks which make great use of parallel construction and anaphora, creating a Biblical rhythm to his words. This rhythm adds to the sense of gravity he is trying to import. He proceeds to imagine what Bigger must have thought during his crimes and accuses him of raping Mary, a crime sure to rouse the mob to anger and violence. Interestingly, the actual rape of Bessie takes a distant second stage because Bessie was a black woman, though she is invoked to show how cold-blooded a murderer Bigger was thought to be. Buckley concludes by demanding the death penalty. Despite Max's protestations for more time, the court adjourns for an hour before rendering its decision.

Max and Bigger spend the hour together in his cell. The court reconvenes and the judge says that the court's duty is clear based on the feeling of the people—Bigger will be put to death. He is returned to his cell where Max tries to comfort him, saying he will appeal to the governor, but Bigger rebuffs him. In the days that follow, Bigger tells his visiting family to go home and forget him. A priest tries to make him pray; Bigger flings coffee in his face. He finally decides that the only person he wants to see again is Max. Though he did not fully understand Max's courtroom speech, Bigger felt stronger for it, as if he had feeling and meaning. He wants to rekindle that in speech with Max; he wants to know why he hesitates to die in spite of everything that has been bad in his life. He is filled with a persistent wonder. On the day of the execution, he receives a message from Max confirming that nothing more can be done. Bigger spends the afternoon on his cot until he is awakened by Max's visit.

Max tries to offer him comfort, and Bigger tries to think about how to articulate all that he is feeling despite the fear that he will be unable to finally voice what he feels. Max, knowing Bigger wants to talk, tries to coax the words from him, but Bigger remains unable to translate his thoughts. He feels that ability was denied him, as he lived as an outsider to men and their modes of communication. Finally, Bigger tells Max that he was glad to know him, glad that Max asked him all of the questions about himself. Max cannot recall the questions Bigger refers too and the young man feels betrayed, as if Max never knew him. Bigger tries to explain that the questions were the first time that anyone ever treated Bigger like a man, an equal. Max continues to try to comfort Bigger, not understanding that Bigger also resented the questions as they made him think and brought him hope. That lifting of a veil makes Bigger incredulous that now he has to die. Still, determined to talk, he tries to explain to Max that he lashed out because he felt penned in, attacked, and that in reality he is not hard. He is broken and sad that he never saw the people around him for who they were, white or black, and they never saw him. He works through the thought that maybe the people who want him dead are striving for something too and they will realize after his death that, like Bigger, they never meant to hurt anyone either. Max resists telling the truth, not wanting to hurt Bigger or give him false hope. Max calls Bigger to the window to look at the buildings of the city which he claims are held together by the belief of man; the same feeling that drove Bigger to want to do something. That desire, Max says, keeps things progressing, but now the men inside the buildings doubt the power, and the men that own the buildings simply want to hold onto their assets. The world stagnates. Max claims that other men are coming now who want more, who want to tear down the buildings, the existing social structure and build something new that can accommodate change. Bigger mumbles that he always wanted to do something too, but Max tells him that he will never do that. Bigger will die, but he has the choice to die free, to believe in himself in spite of all of the hate that surrounds him. Max begins to stutter the words and Bigger bursts out laughing, breaking the intimacy between them. He tells Max that faith in himself is all he's got, and then he tells Max to go home. But before Max leaves, Bigger finally bursts out with what he wanted to say—though he knows that killing is bad, he finally began to understand who he was and what he wanted after that action.

Bigger exclaims, "What I killed for must've been good! ... When a man kills, it's for something ... I didn't know I was really alive in this world until I felt things hard enough to kill for 'em ... (429)" His outburst terrifies Max, but it calms the conviction in Bigger. When Max turns to leave, Bigger tells him not to worry, that he will be okay. As Max walks out, Bigger yells out again, telling Max to say hello to Jan.

Significantly, he does not use Jan's surname; instead, he calls to him as a friend, an equal. The book ends with the distant clang of a door closing, a suitable metaphor for the end that looms beyond the pages.

Critical Views

AIMÉ J. ELLIS ON PLAYING TOUGH AND MASCULINE BRAVADO

For Bigger and his South Side Chicago cronies, Doc's poolroom afforded the daily opportunity to congregate, relax, kill time, escape the drudgery of looking for hard-to-get menial jobs and plot illegal ventures to acquire fast money.[14] A world unto itself, Doc's poolroom symbolized a site of black male community that stood as a testing ground for measuring one's manhood and courage in the midst of perpetual racial assault and terror. The poolroom scene in *Native Son* centers around an ambitious if not outlandish scheme: Bigger and his gang would rob Blum's delicatessen, a small neighborhood store owned and run by a Jewish man. For Bigger, Gus, and their two running partners, G. H. and Jack, robbing Blum's represented the ultimate test of defiant oppositionality and rebellion. Wright observes,

> They had always robbed Negroes. They felt that it was much easier and safer to rob their own people, for they knew that white policemen never really searched diligently for Negroes who committed crimes against other Negroes. For months they had talked of robbing Blum's, but had not been able to bring themselves to do it. They had the feeling that the robbing of Blum's would be a violation of ultimate taboo; it would be a trespassing into territory where the full wrath of an alien white world would be turned loose upon them; in short, it would be a symbolic challenge of the white world's rule over them; a challenge which they yearned to make, but were afraid to. Yes; if they could rob Blum's, it would be a real hold-up, in more senses than one. In comparison, all of their other jobs had been play. (*NS* 14)

That Bigger and his male friends "robbed Negroes" as a way to survive the harsh Depression era of Chicago's South Side is a clear illustration of Bigger's detachment from and disregard for black communal harmony. Yet robbing and stealing allowed Bigger and his friends to painstakingly challenge systematic black disenfranchisement as well as to "resist wage labor, pursue leisure, and demystify the work ethic myth" (Kelley 176). But their "criminal" acts would also pose other challenges to both themselves and the larger social order.

For Bigger and his friends, stealing from whites, unlike from blacks, represented a "symbolic challenge to the white world's rule over them" (*NS* 14).[15] Psychologically, the challenge of robbing a white-owned store—especially those white establishments within the Black Belt—constituted for Bigger and his friends the site of a phantasmal liberation from white domination. In effect, the project of defiantly opposing the status quo of Jim Crow (i.e., robbing a white-owned store) becomes itself a male rite of passage, a passage representing the process through which Bigger and his male friends attempt to assert their humanity. In this instance, it is their ability to conquer what they fear most, to assert a sense of fearlessness and defiance that becomes tantamount to black male empowerment. Indeed, as Keith Clark rightly asserts in his critique of Wright's protest discourse, "Black manhood is achieved only by standing up to white men" (81).

What this scene suggests, however, is that fearlessness exists as a psychic ideal to which Bigger and his friends can only approximate through masking their fears and "playing tough." That this ideal involves an assertion of masculine bravado and, for Bigger, the projection of violent behavior onto his buddies problematically constitutes both hypermasculinity and fearlessness as sites of empowerment, status, and self-worth.[16] That is to say, fearlessness is empowering because it frees Bigger of his inferiority complex and functions to restore his self-respect. However, it is also debilitating and, indeed, destructive because it violently works to threaten communal harmony as well as to disrupt the black male community it purports to nurture. Take, for example, Bigger's desperate exhibition of brute force over Gus when Gus exposes Bigger's fear of going through with the robbery:

> "Lick it," Bigger said, his body tingling with elation. Gus's eyes filled with tears. "Lick it, I said! You think I'm playing?" Gus looked round the room without moving his head, just rolling his eyes in a mute appeal for help. But no one moved. Bigger's left fist was slowly lifting to strike. Gus's lips moved toward the knife; he stuck out his tongue and touched the blade. Gus's lips quivered and tears streamed down his cheeks. (*NS* 39)

In this scene Bigger violently forces Gus to "lick" his knife, a symbol of Bigger's penis. Filled with "elation" as Gus demeans himself by performing the symbolic act of fellatio on Bigger in front of his male peers, Bigger "rapes" Gus to assert his "power" over him. Here it seems crucial to call attention to the sexualized dimensionality of these homosocial practices, practices that employ both physical and sexual violence in a desperate effort to regain lost masculinity. As Mercer rightly points out in his analysis of sexualized violence among black men,

> The kind of "power" acted out in the brutal violence of rape and sexual abuse is, in fact, a further expression of powerlessness, as it does nothing to challenge the underlying structure of oppression, but only "passes on" the violence of the dominant white male, via the psychic process of internalization, into the black community and onto black women [and men], hence reinforcing their oppression at the end of the chain of colonial violence. (146)

Masking their fears by playing tough is thus a kind of desperate assertion that ultimately never succeeds in freeing Bigger and his friends from psychological bondage and intraracial discord. Nevertheless, it is the assertion itself of defiant oppositionality and hypermasculinity—and the perceived need for that assertion—that becomes both the site of and occasion for grappling with their humanity; indeed, these two factors coalesce to produce the mobilizing energy around which black male community is created and sustained. Described by Cornel West as "black male bonding networks that flaunt machismo [and] promote camaraderie," the homosocial exchanges between young black males in black culture in general and in the first book of *Native Son* in particular symbolize not only a site of racial community but also function as a space for cultivating male rites of passage that solicit self-affirmation and respect (27). On the one hand, these hypermasculinist and often sexualized practices amounted to hyperbolic appropriations of white male authority within the segregated social and cultural sphere of black life during the 1930s; on the other, homosocial networks of black male community, particularly those defined within and against Jim Crow, challenged and even incited confrontation with white society as a way to both express resistance and to preserve their humanity against racial and class oppression.

Notes

14. The unlikely prospect of landing menial jobs was often referred to as a situation in which blacks were "forced to 'only stand and wait' at relief stations, on street corners, in poolrooms and taverns, in policy stations and churches, for opportunities that never came and for the work which eluded both them and their white fellow-hopers" (Cayton and Drake 523).

15. Wright's reference to antagonist black–Jewish relations in *Native Son* is supported by the violent anti-Semitic campaign of 1938. According to Horace Cayton, Jr., and St. Clair Drake in *Black Metropolis: A Study of Negro Life in a Northern City* (1945), "The inhabitants of the Black Ghetto grow restless in their frustration, penned in, isolated, overcrowded. During a depression or a war (the periods covered by this account), the consciousness of their exclusion and subordination is tremendously heightened. Within this spatial and social framework morale tends to be low and tempers taut. Anti-Semitic sentiments are latent" (213).

16. bell hooks writes in *Killing Rage: Ending Racism* (1995): "Within black life, as well as in mainstream society, males prove they are 'men' by the exhibition of antisocial behavior, lack of consideration for the needs of others, refusal to communicate, unwillingness to show

nurturance and care. Here I am not speaking about traits adult males cultivate, I am talking about the traits little boys learn early in life to associate with manhood and act out" (74).

MICHAEL BÉRUBÉ ON THE TRIAL

It's worth noting that Max's insistence on Bigger as symbol, like his insinuation that Bigger needs to be brought within the ambit of "civilization," is uncomfortably similar to the rhetorical strategies employed by the prosecution.[3] But in the recent past I have begun class discussion otherwise, by pointing out that Max's plea of guilty in Bigger's case is as questionable a legal strategy as that employed by the defense in Mike Tyson's 1992 rape trial. The Tyson-Bigger intertext is, of course, both rich and volatile. Just as Tyson's defense team argued that their client was so notoriously unstable and dangerous, so Bigger-like, that no prudent woman would meet him alone at midnight, so too does Max start from the premise that Bigger must be established as pathological. Though Max adopts this line of defense in order to argue that Bigger is but a symptom of a larger national pathology, he never challenges the prosecution's charge of rape. As in the Tyson trial, the "defense" explains why the bigger bad-nigger acts the way he does instead of attempting to sow the seeds of reasonable doubt in the minds of the jurors. The gender politics of both defense strategies are similar, too, and similarly odious. Where the Tyson team blames the woman, Max ignores Bigger's killing of Bessie.

The classic critique of Max's strategy was formulated by Benjamin Davis Jr. in the *Sunday Worker* of 14 April 1940, where he notes that if Max were truly an ILD lawyer, he would have contested the charge that Bigger raped Mary, would have dealt with the murder of Bessie, and would have entered a plea of not guilty.[4] Davis himself was an African American official in the Communist Party, so his critique is something of a partisan review. But his was the only contemporary review of the novel to take Max's speech seriously for its legal and propositional content and one of the few reviews to register outrage that Bessie's murder is of no moment to the court—no moment because, as Bigger himself knew, "white people did not really care about Bessie's being killed.... He had even heard it said that white people felt it was good when one Negro killed another; it meant that they had one Negro less to contend with" (383). More recent commentators have pointed out that Max's defense "speaks for" Bigger in the manner in which white Americans have long represented blackness to one another. As Robert Stepto puts it, "While transcending the character type in the slave narratives which he first resembles, Max soon takes on the features of a familiar turn-of-the-century type, the 'white moral voice'" ("I Thought" 632).[5] In other words, Max may not be representative of the ILD or the Communist Party, but he may plausibly be said to represent the figure of the sympathetic white man who doesn't quite understand the widespread racial unrest of which he speaks. In this respect I have sometimes thought that Max might be an uncomfortable analogue for my own position in the classroom—even though Bigger's life does not depend on whether I persuade my students that my interpretation is plausible.

State's Attorney Buckley employs a rather different sense of representation. He has no interest in trying to depict Bigger faithfully; his declaration, instead, is that he, Buckley, represents the people. His opening statement makes this point in histrionic fashion. On surveying the courtroom crowd, Buckley cries, "It is not often ... that a representative of the people finds the masses of the citizens who elected him to office standing literally at his back, waiting for him to enforce the law" (433). Having thus identified their clients, Buckley and Max square off for the right to frame Bigger's representation. *Native Son* begins to represent itself in astonishingly minute detail, as the novel basically retells its first hundred pages from the perspectives of Buckley, Max, and the court officials who recite "over and over" the charges that Bigger raped and killed both Bessie and Mary (429). One might say, in fact, that the function of the entire legal apparatus in *Native Son* is to retell *Native Son*, for no sooner is Mary's disappearance discovered than Bigger has to listen to people like Britten, the private eye, "tell the story all over again" (240).

Accordingly, the novel's third section is heavily, even obsessively, repetitive. Though Bigger declines to reenact the crime at the Dalton house, for instance, Buckley reenacts it in the courtroom, and he calls to the stand sixty witnesses, including sixteen police officers, fifteen newspapermen, six doctors, five handwriting analysts, five psychiatrists, and four black waitresses. No doubt many readers have had reason to agree with Morris Dickstein that the novel's conclusion amounts to little more than a "curious but inert ideological essay," an "immensely long and disappointing coda" (161). If readers are looking for suspense, horror, and rooftop chases, *Native Son*'s trial scene can only be a disappointment.

But in my reading, the point of the trial is precisely to represent the novel. One would think that Buckley's sixty witnesses were sufficient to try the case; but he proceeds to comb through the novel for each of the artifacts relevant to Bigger's crimes.

> Buckley brought forth the knife and purse Bigger had hidden in the garbage pail [on pages 111–12] and informed the Court that the city's dump had been combed for four days to find them. The brick he had used to strike Bessie with was shown; then came the flashlight, the Communist pamphlets, the gun, the blackened earring, the hatchet blade, the signed confession, the kidnap note, Bessie's bloody clothes, the stained pillows and quilts, the trunk, and the empty rum bottle which had been found in the snow near a curb. (441)

The novel's opening pages depict workmen plastering Bigger's neighborhood with a campaign poster for Buckley, a poster that features "one of those faces that looked straight at you when you looked at it and all the while you were walking and turning your head to look at it it kept looking unblinkingly back at you" (12–13). It's safe to say, given the above inventory, that the poster is a "true" representation, that it really works:

apparently, Buckley and the Chicago police can see everything Bigger does and can represent it to themselves for their own purposes.[6] In court, having presented their witnesses and represented the novel's data, they then stage what's now called a "dramatic reenactment" of Bigger's attempt to burn Mary's body, using the furnace itself rather than a replica:

> [A] group of twelve workmen brought in the furnace, piece by piece, from the Dalton basement and mounted it upon a giant wooden platform.... Buckley had a white girl [!], the size of Mary, crawl inside the furnace "to prove beyond doubt that it could and did hold and burn the ravished body of innocent Mary Dalton; and to show that the poor girl's head could not go in and the sadistic Negro cut it off." (441–42)

Fortunately for Mary's understudy, Buckley does not pursue strict verisimilitude this once.

The state's powers of surveillance are by no means limited to the accumulation of material objects; Buckley, like a hyperrealist novelist, can also make a narrative of his evidence. He claims, disingenuously, that he will be sullied by the very narration of the story: "[L]iterally I shrink from the mere recital of this dastardly crime. I cannot speak of it without feeling somehow contaminated by the mere telling of it" (476–77). Despite his sense of contamination, he proceeds to retell Bigger's story for some seven pages, disclosing along the way that he even knows that Bigger "did not want to work" (477) and had "consented only when his mother informed him that the relief would cut off their supply of food if he did not accept" (478; his mother had complained to Bigger, "even when the relief offers you a job you won't take it till they threaten to cut off your food" [7]).

Wright's immediate point, certainly, has to do with the extent to which residents of Chicago's South Side are living in a police state, where the mental and physical contents of their lives may be dragged into the public sphere and represented by the state for the purpose of incarcerating or killing them. It's quite clear that the conditions of ghetto life, in *Native Son* as in the United States, amount to a form of psychological terrorism. The anger Bigger feels in court is the anger of the captive, "an old feeling that Bessie had often described to him when she had come from long hours of hot toil in the white folks' kitchens, a feeling of being forever commanded by others so much that thinking and feeling for one's self was impossible" (383). It's fitting, therefore, that Buckley be such an omniscient, if unsympathetic, narrator. But then what's odd about the trial in *Native Son* is that Max's representation also performs a kind of psychological surveillance of Bigger, likewise displaying the details of Bigger's interiority to the court. If Max were having Bigger plead innocent, there would be little wrong with this; Max is performing an affirmative task simply in demonstrating to the court that Bigger has an interiority—that he is not, as Buckley, would have it, a "half-human black ape" (476), a "black lizard" (476), or a "demented savage" (483). But since Max ultimately pleads for Bigger's imprisonmment, there's something deeply unsettling about Max's ability to represent Bigger's innermost thoughts while Bigger remains mute.

In the first section of the novel, for instance, the narrator writes: "To Bigger and his kind white people were not really people; they were a sort of great natural force, like a stormy sky looming overhead, or like a deep swirling river stretching suddenly at one's feet in the dark" (129). Over three hundred pages later, Max knows, as surely as if he had already read *Native Son*, that people such as Bigger "feel that they are facing mountains, floods, seas: forces of nature" (450). As we were told that Bigger "had killed many times before" (119, 277), so does Max know that "he has murdered many times" (466); as we heard that "these two murders were the most meaningful things that had ever happened to him" (277), so does Max know that Mary's murder "was the most meaningful, exciting and stirring thing that had ever happened to him" (461).

Notes
3. Likewise, both attorneys figure the South Side as a jungle: where Max speaks of Bigger in the "wild forest of our great cities, amid the rank and choking vegetation of slums" (456), Buckley calls for the

judge "to tell [the people] that jungle law does not prevail in this city" (483). Needless to say, the jungle imagery tends to work better for Buckley. Reilly notes a correspondence between Buckley's accounts and the narrative voice of the novel: "The racist versions of Bigger's story bear crucial resemblance to the summary statements of his psychology related early in the novel, out of intimate knowledge, by the presiding narrative voice" ("Giving" 52).

4. Davis's summary of Max's performance is severe: "He argues that Bigger, and by implication the whole Negro mass, should be held in jail to protect 'white daughters' though capitalism is plainly the guilty criminal which threatens poor white womanhood as well as Negro.... From Max's whole conduct the first business of the Communist Party or of the I.L.D. would have been to chuck him out of the case" (Reilly, *Richard Wright* 75).

5. Keneth Kinnamon makes a similar argument with regard to Wright's negotiations with his editor, Edward Aswell, suggesting that Aswell "may even be regarded as standing in relation to Wright as Max stands in relation to Bigger: sympathetic, loyal, analytical, understanding to a point, but not quite ready to accept the full and uncut expression of a sensibility so radically different from his own" (Introduction 16). On a related note, Kinnamon also proposes that Fisher's introduction to *Native Son* is "a latter-day example of the process of white authentication which Robert Stepto has shown to be so characteristic a feature of slave narratives" (17).

6. Buckley astonishes Bigger when he reveals that he knows about the planned robbery of Blum's store; Buckley also knows that Bigger and his friend Jack masturbated in the Regal Theatre (354).

MICHAEL FABRE ON THE SIGNIFICANCE OF THE WHITE WOMAN

Let's return to our beginning key scene and to the suffocation of Mary in her bedroom in order to emphasize the role of descriptive details. Whether cave or basement, the place where combustibles are stored corresponds to the lower regions of the subconscious, to the deepest instincts; the bedroom (the woman's room) is a sanctuary defiled by Bigger's intrusion at Mary's house and by Richard's at Mrs. Bibbs' house. In most of the scenes of this type the intrusion is really a violent invasion of the bedroom and emphasizes the voyeuristic position of the intruder. Leaving aside for the time being the child who sees a couple making love, note that to surprise a nude white woman (or inversely, to allow oneself to be surprised nude by her as in "Big Boy Leaves Home") signifies the risk of being accused of rape and being lynched. The narrator explicitly makes this known in *Native Son*, "The Man Who Killed A Shadow", and *The Long Dream*—and the plot often corroborates their fears. In *The Long Dream*, the sheriff goes so far as to employ a white woman to accuse Fishbelly of rape. This fear is always present in the protagonist's mind as it is in the novelist's. Other fictional confrontations are only in some way variations of this situation where the black man is put in danger by the white woman. The reaction of the latter is infallible: she holds back her breath before crying, and the cry, when it is uttered, sounds like an inhuman howl signing the black's death warrant. "The Man Who Killed a Shadow" offers the most typical example of this:

> She sucked in her breath, sprang up, and stepped away from him. Then she screamed sharply, and her voice was like a lash cutting into his chest. She screamed again and he backed away from her. He felt helpless, strange.... In her scream he heard the sirens of the police cars that hunted down black men.... This woman was screaming as though he had raped her (pp. 201–6).

The same reaction occurs in "The Man Who Lived Underground" when the office-worker perceives Daniels: "He tiptoed to a door and eased it open. A fair-haired white girl stood in front of a steel cabinet, her blue eyes wide upon him. She turned chalky and gave a high-pitched scream." (p. 50)

If, in *Native Son*, Mary is drunk and cannot cry out, her mother could, which causes the crazy terror of Bigger, who suffocates the girl. Other situations invert or vary the context of the episode. In "Down by the Riverside", it is the Heartfield son who, the symbolic protector of his mother, cries out in recognizing the murderer of his father. Although Mann merely defended himself, this murder entailed a potentially sexual menace toward white women, and Mann's bursting into the Heartfield house, even if to save the survivors, connotes rape. Equally, in "Big Boy Leaves Home," the situation seems inverted since it is black adolescents who swim nude. Their astonishment can be read, in fact, like a reflex of modesty: "It's a woman, whispered Big Boy in an underbreath, a *white* woman. They started, their hands instinctively covering their groins. Then they scrambled to their feet. The white woman backed slowly out of sight" (*UTC*, p. 36). Some lines later, it is the woman who is afraid: "The woman, her eyes wide, her hand over her mouth, backed away to the tree where their clothes lay in a heap" (*UTC*, p. 27). Though justified by the narrative context, these descriptions also serve to reproduce the trauma of young Wright's unintentionally breaking the prohibition which surrounds white women, to such an extent that the writer seems committed, whether by conscious recourse or at a more symbolic and almost archetypical level of black/white confrontation, to reproduce this situation. Beyond race, the encounter is anchored in a sexual taboo. In fact, the racial prohibition which surrounds the white woman is coupled with the social prohibition which surrounds the mother, whose form, as we have seen, seems to be divided in two: she is at once the young woman whom the little boy dreams of possessing and the older person who incarnates the voice of conscience.

For Wright, the mother in this second sense is associated with the character of the grandmother. Mrs. Dalton is not an old woman, but her white hair, hieratic bearing, and carefully measured walk evidence an already aged woman. One thinks of Mrs. Bibbs' mother, a background presence in the house, but also, quite evidently, of Richard's grandmother who seems to reappear periodically, for example, in the character of Granny in "Down by the Riverside." This ancestor, the voice of the conscience, is associated so much more easily with whiteness and with prohibition since, in reality, as stated in the beginning of *Black Boy*, "Mrs. Wilson was white as any 'white' person" (p. 21), as revealed by her "white grim face framed by a halo of tumbling black hair" in her bedroom of long muslin curtains.

Whiteness, authority, and frozen purity are associated. In any case it seems that a moral crime against a woman is often framed in curtains, feathers, and light fluffy immaculate fabric. We are thus tempted to take as significant the decor of the grandmother's bedroom, long fluffy white curtains.... huge feather pillow" (*BB*, p. 3), which corresponds to a transgression of a major prohibition (to play with fire) and to a traumatic, long-lasting and far-reaching reprimand received from Mrs. Wright. In one of the crucial scenes of *Native Son*, the importance of a fluffy decor in the unreal light of dawn was so evident that it inspired the production of Orson Welles: "shadowy form of a white bed.... hazy blue light.... the furtive gleam of her white teeth.... a white blur was standing by the door, silent, ghostlike" (pp. 73). In this episode, the pillow is going to play a role as essential as in *Othello*; but whether or not the reference to Shakespeare is certain, the pillow will be found in similar contexts. When Bigger goes out on to the street to confront the blizzard, it seems that an enormous pillow was opened out of which snow swirls in the cold wind. As a correlative object, the blizzard outside is a transposition of a sack of feathers which, like Bigger in the room, were "ready to explode." In a rough draft of the autobiography, the grandmother's room is not only garnished with white curtains but full of pillows, those on which grandmother rests and those in a clothes closet: I go to the clothes closet, climb on top of a soft pile of pillows and quilts, curl up and try to sleep" ("Black Yesterdays", Wright Archives, Yale University Library). In an unforgettable way, the pillow, like the whirlwind of feathers turns out to be tied to Bobo's lynching in "Big Boy Leaves Home": "He shrank violently as the wind carried, like a flurry of snow, a widening spiral of white feathers into the night. The flames leaped tall as the trees" (*UTC*, p. 62).

SONDRA GUTTMAN ON MARY'S DEATH

The blind Mrs. Dalton is referred to repeatedly throughout *Native Son* as a ghost, and at this moment her entrance into Mary's room is characteristically described as "ghostlike" (97). Mrs. Dalton represents the haunting negative of Mary—the not-quite-obsolete exemplar of white ladyhood as described in the previous quote from Jacquelyn Dowd Hall. As if to remind Mary of her proper place, Mrs. Dalton is the ghostly, disembodied, intrusion of convention. Bigger's fear of the conventional treatment of black men caught in situations like his, then, explains his need to silence Mary at this moment. As Bigger reacts to Mrs. Dalton's presence, his desire to do violence becomes indistinguishable from sexual desire:

> Mary mumbled and tried to rise again. Frantically, he caught a corner of the pillow and brought it to her lips. He had to stop her from mumbling, or he would be caught. Mrs. Dalton was moving slowly toward him and he grew tight and full, as though about to explode. Mary's fingernails tore at his hands and he caught the pillow and covered her entire face with it, firmly. Mary's body surged upward and he pushed downward upon the pillow with all of his weight (97–98).

In contradistinction to the previous moments in which Bigger and Mary had moved together in the No Man's Land of consensual union, now Bigger's and Mary's bodies are locked back into the dialectic of place—of above and below. As Mary attempts to rise up and to reoccupy her position above him, Bigger must force her body down. It is at this moment, when Bigger, feeling "tight and full, as though about to explode," presses "all of his weight" onto Mary's upwardly surging body that Wright's description invokes rape.

It is important to point out that while Bigger does not rape Mary, Wright's portrayal of Mary's murder is replete with sexual imagery and sexual tension. Bigger and Mary are sexually engaged when Mrs. Dalton enters the room. As Bigger suffocates Mary, his actions are described in sexual terms. Though Mary's death can indeed be seen as accidental in the sense that Bigger does not intend to kill her, the sexualized portrayal of the scene suggests that Mary's death is, to a certain extent, predetermined by the race-class system—a system maintained by ideological narratives that sexualize racial difference. This is a murder that would not have happened had

Bigger not perceived himself in imminent danger when caught in a white woman's room. In that sense, it is no simple accident. The scene continues:

> He could see Mrs. Dalton plainly now. As he took his hands from the pillow he heard a long slow sigh go up from the bed into the air of the darkened room, a sigh which afterwards, when he remembered it, seemed final, irrevocable.... With each of [Mrs. Dalton's] movements toward the bed his body made a movement to match hers, away from her. (98)

Ultimately, it is Mary's death, her final "long slow sigh," that irrevocably reinstates these bodies into their traditional places. Once Bigger has fulfilled the role that the myth demands of him, once he has killed Mary, Mrs. Dalton replaces her daughter and hegemony is reestablished. The bodies of the black man and the white woman are again opposed. Bigger's negative enactment of Mrs. Dalton's movements mimic this reinstatement.

FARAH JASMINE GRIFFIN CONTRASTS THE MURDERS OF MARY AND BESSIE

The city sends the male migrant mixed messages. It provides him the space to fantasize about and helps him construct his desire for a world to which it denies him access. White women, representative of this world, are the vehicle through which it is accessed. Bigger the migrant brings with him from the South the taboo of interracial sex and the fear of acting on his desire, yet the city teases him by allowing a modicum of psychic space for his fantasies.

It is the fantasy and the fear that Bigger takes with him into the Dalton's home. Fear and desire fill the novel's first murder. He puts the drunken Mary to bed: "[H]e leaned over her, excited, looking at her face in the dim light, not wanting to take his hands from her breasts. She tossed and mumbled sleepily. He tightened his fingers on her breasts, kissing her again, feeling her move toward him" (96–97). Bigger has the courage to act on his sexual desire for Mary because she is only slightly conscious. It is a secret moment for him, one that many of my students call a rape because he touches her without her consent. Wright does not write the scene as a rape; in fact, he implies Mary's consent. In these days of heightened awareness about date rape, I find that more and more of my students see this touching as the rape of Mary Dalton. In class discussion students may not only express anger at Bigger but also challenge Wright on the validity of a drunken woman's consent. This scene might be one of the first moments of the book where Wright is implicated in sexism. Of course, there will be students who agree that Mary desires Bigger as well. But Bigger has a position of relative power and authority at this point: Mary's safety is in his hands.

His momentary possession of power and desire is immediately disrupted and replaced with fear when Mrs. Dalton enters the room. Fear and desire culminate in the enactment of a murder that is described in sexual terms:

> Frenzy dominated him.... Frantically, he caught a corner of the pillow and brought it to her lips.... Mary's fingernails tore at his hands and he caught the pillow and covered her entire face with it, firmly. Mary's body surged upward and he pushed downward upon the pillow with all of his weight.... Mary's body heaved.... He clenched his teeth and held his breath.... His muscles flexed taut as steel and he pressed the pillow, feeling the bed give slowly, evenly, but silently.... He relaxed and sank to the floor, his breath going in a long gasp. He was weak and wet with sweat.... Gradually, the intensity of his sensations subsided.... (97–99)

Unable to act on his sexual desire through intercourse, Bigger does so through violence—violence precipitated by the fear of being caught with a white woman. Mary is desirable to him because she provides access to the rights and privileges of a fantasy world constructed by the cinema. Unable to possess her, he kills her.

This murder is in stark contrast to the murder of Bigger's black girlfriend, Bessie Mears. When Bigger acts on his sexual desire for Bessie, it is a blatant rape. There is no consent; Bessie struggles and repeatedly says no. Yet he takes her violently, because her body is the only space where he can enact unbridled agency and authority. Shortly after her rape, he decides he must kill her because only she can identify him as the murderer of Mary Dalton.

Bigger murders Bessie not in response to desire but in order to be rid of her. Bessie threatens to thwart his potential. She knows of his crime and, like all black women in Wright's texts, binds him to an inhibiting racial past. Bigger murders her not out of fear but out of the wish to be free.

> Then he took a deep breath and his hand gripped the brick and shot upward and paused a second and then plunged downward through the darkness to the accompaniment of a deep short grunt from his chest and landed with a thud. Yes! There was a dull gasp of surprise, then a moan. No, that must not be! He lifted the brick again and again, until in falling it struck a sodden mass that gave softly but stoutly to each landing blow. Soon he seemed to be striking a wet wad of cotton, of some damp substance whose only life was the jarring of the brick's impact. He stopped, hearing his own breath heaving in and out of his chest. He was wet all over, and cold. How many times he had lifted the brick and brought it down he did not know. All he knew was that the room was quiet and cold and that the job was done. (274)

It is significant that this murder takes place in the book titled "Flight." Bessie's death is a prerequisite to Bigger's freedom. The language describing her murder is not the language of desire and lovemaking; it is the violent sexual language of a rape. The rape precedes the murder, and the murder itself is an act of rape, a violation and destruction of a black woman.

Bigger is not acting out of fear here; he kills Bessie out of hate—hate for what she as a black woman represents to him. Unlike Mary, she is not the future to which he aspires but the past from which he flees.

Though Wright is critical of Bigger's murdering Bessie, he seems to share Bigger's view of the black woman as a fetter, as a chain to the provincial past. There is no evidence that Wright is aware of the mechanisms that shape this perspective. While he details the elements of the dominant society that construct Bigger's desire for Mary, he does not detail those elements that construct Bigger's disdain for Bessie. Nor does Wright give the reasons why Bessie or Mrs. Thomas lives in a state of resignation. (Ann Petry, Wright's contemporary, gives reasons for resignation in her novel *The Street*. I usually assign it immediately following *Native Son*.) Although Wright is adept at revealing the social sources of Bigger's sexual attitudes, he has not escaped this socialization in his own life.

Just as Bigger sacrifices the lives of Mary and Bessie for his fear and freedom, so does Wright. Neither woman is given the complexity or depth of Bigger; they exist only to demonstrate Bigger's aspirations and inhibitions. Their murders and the following attempts to flee the police are the only instances where Bigger is allowed any agency. It is through these murders that he gains a heightened critical consciousness.

CAREN IRR ON BIGGER'S CLAUSTROPHOBIA

The major psychological pattern that Wright traces is claustrophobic anxiety. By way of revising the map of culture proposed in the proletarian novel, *Native Son* manifests symptoms of a fear of enclosure; then, it briefly becomes agoraphobic, until it finally relapses into an enhanced, even utopian, form of spatial anxiety. These phobic effects are produced cumulatively, as well as in particular symbolic details, but recreating the flow of Wright's narrative should clarify some of the unique features of his political and literary practice.

Native Son begins with depictions of enclosed spaces and the psychology of living in them. Readers of *12 Million Black Voices*, Wright's "folk history" of African American life, immediately recognize that the spaces portrayed in the first pages of the novel are those that Wright considered typical of the limited circuit of African American urban life: the kitchenette, the pool room, and the movie theater.[10] In these initial settings, Wright establishes the kernel of his novel; he sketches the phobias that organize the novel and exhibit its implicit critique of the proletarian novel.

The "narrow space" of the kitchenette is one of the novel's most significant locations.[11] In the first scene, Wright uses the closeness of this space to establish a clear parallel between the two Thomas boys and a rat they trap in a corner of the apartment. His mother tells Bigger to "'Put that box in front of the hole so [the rat] can't get out!'" (p. 9). This command is then transferred to Bigger, when she repeatedly threatens him: "'if you don't like it, you can get out'" (p. 13). Of course, both comments function ironically, since neither Bigger nor the rat can "get out." Bigger cannot escape from his family or from a sense of responsibility for his family. Like the rat, Bigger wants "a wider choice of action" but does not have it (p. 16). Both of them are cornered in the kitchenette.

To cope with his feeling of entrapment, Bigger places himself "behind a wall, a curtain" (p. 14). This self-imposed isolation is a personal version of the ritual his family has developed to preserve their collective modesty while dressing; Bigger figuratively turns his head aside to create the kind of privacy he desires. This seemingly passive withdrawal is not, however, the only element of Bigger's ritual; when he begins to fear his own entrapment, he also violently displaces that fear. In the kitchenette scene, this displacement has two stages. First, Bigger kills the rat with an excessive amount of force; he distances himself from his fear by hysterically overacting a version of it. Then he uses the evidence of his compensatory violence to frighten his "scary" sister (p. 10). The word "scary" is clearly important in this passage, since it is repeated several times and is one of the first colloquialisms used in the novel.[12]

These two items suggest that Vera is not only easily frightened but also that she is "scary" to Bigger and that part of his purpose in killing the rat was to slaughter and displace his fear of her. Being trapped in the kitchenette involves, for Bigger, being forced into an oppressive and repressed awareness of the proximity of the black female body, and he responds to that body (as represented by his sister) with anger and fear. This at least is one of the novel's initial answers to Vera's question "How come Bigger acts that way?" (p. 12).

The psychological pattern established in the kitchenette scene recurs in the following scenes in the poolroom, and only a few elements are altered. Although all the pool players are male and Bigger's victim in this scene is his buddy Gus, not Vera, Bigger again violently displaces his fear of enclosure. Again, his anger takes an object (Gus or the rat) that seems a substitute for something else. In the poolroom scenes, this something else receives a name: race. Bigger explicitly attributes his feeling of suffocation and constriction to the "white folks" who live "right down here in [his] stomach" (p. 24). So, once again, we find Bigger being made physically uncomfortable by his proximity to an other. This suggests that Bigger might be eliding his anxieties about women and "white folks"; the two others fill the same position in his pattern of violent response.

However, be this as it may, it is certainly clear that, as in the previous scene, Bigger's anxious response follows on the heels of a thwarted desire for freedom of movement (desire to fly an airplane) and a ritual behavior that is designed to lessen the pain of the thwarted desire (Bigger and his friends playing "'white'"). Also, as in the kitchenette scene, Bigger's displacement of his fear is so excessive, overblown, and neurotic that it prompts others to voice his own desires. After he attacks Gus in the poolroom, he is so concentrated on substituting rage and hate for fear that he deliberately slices the felt of the pool tables. This gratuitous (and therefore psychologically significant) action leads the owner of the pool room to repeat his mother's threat: "'Get out, before I call a cop! ... Get out of here! ... Get out before I shoot you!'" (p. 42). Having once again provoked another to command him to fulfill his desires, Bigger leaves the site of his claustrophobic panic—with some sense of relief.

Notes

10. Richard Wright, *12 Million Black Voices: A Folk History* (1941; rpt. New York: Arno and *New York Times*, 1969).

11. Richard Wright, *Native Son* (1940; New York: Harper & Row, 1968), 7. All further references will appear in the text.

12. For an interesting discussion of Wright's use of dialect, see Lynda Hungerford, "Dialect Representation in *Native Son*," *Language and Style*, 20 (1987): 3–15.

BARBARA JOHNSON ON BIGGER'S RANSOM LETTER

What is it about Bigger that cannot be re(a)d within the perspective of Ma(r)x?

Max's understanding of Bigger's two murders places them squarely within the perspective of economic determinism. As Max tells the court, Bigger kills because other channels of self-expression are closed to him:

> Listen: what Bigger Thomas did early that Sunday morning in the Dalton home and what he did that Sunday night in that empty building was but a tiny aspect of what he had been doing all his life long! He was *living*, only as he knew how, and as we have forced him to live. The actions that resulted in the death of those two women were as instinctive and inevitable as breathing or blinking one's eyes. It was an act of *creation*!

It has often been assumed that Bigger's crimes can therefore be seen as that which, in the novel, stands in the place of *art*. Bigger is an artist with no medium to work in other than violence.

But is this actually the case? It will be my contention that there is in fact, within the novel itself, another sort of "Blueprint for Negro Writing," one that complicates the notion of a creativity "as instinctive and inevitable as breathing or blinking one's eyes" (indeed, one that makes even breathing and blinking the eyes into signifying acts that are not merely instinctual).

For Bigger, in fact, does not merely kill. He also writes. He writes a ransom note to the father of the white woman he has inadvertently killed. That note, and the scene of its writing, can be read in a way that exceeds its contextual function. And the reception of that text turns out to be as telling as its creation.

The scene of writing begins with the silencing of Bessie, the black woman whose involvement with Bigger will soon prove fatal to her.

> "I ain't asking you but once more to shut up!" he said, pushing the knife out of the way so he could write.

Substituting the pencil for the knife, Bigger performs an elaborate ritual of concealment, self-protection, and disguise:

> He put on the gloves and took up the pencil in a trembling hand and held it poised over the paper. He should disguise his handwriting. He changed the pencil from his right to his left hand. He would not write it; he would print it. He swallowed with dry throat.

Bigger's writing is designed to betray no trace of origin or signature. He is then faced with the question of pronoun: is his writing to be individual or collective? This is indeed the question Richard Wright has put before the Negro writer who wishes to write on the "left."

> Now, what would be the best kind of note? He thought, I want you to put ten thousand.... Naw; that would not do. Not "I." It would be better to say "we."

Instead of proceeding directly to his demand ("I want you to put ten thousand...."), Bigger now makes up a story for the benefit of the addressee, the white male reader, leading with what he knows to be Mr. Dalton's concern:

> *We got your daughter*, he printed slowly in big round letters. That was better. He ought to say something to let Mr. Dalton think that Mary was still alive. He wrote: *She is safe*. Now, tell him not to go to the police. No! Say something about Mary first! He bent and wrote: *She wants to come home....*

As he continues the note, he makes a crucial textual revision:

> Now, tell him not to go to the police. *Don't go to the police if you want your daughter back safe*. Naw; that ain't good. His scalp tingled with excitement; it seemed that he could feel each strand of hair upon his head. He read the line over and crossed out "safe" and wrote "alive."

What Bigger's visceral reaction demonstrates is his knowledge that his own fate is bound to the way in which his writing is linked, in the implied reader's mind, with the fate of a white woman. It is precisely Bigger's belief in the white father's inability to think his daughter safe that has led to her not being alive in the first place. Bigger implicitly feels the significance of his revision and all that needs to be revised behind it:

> For a moment he was frozen, still. There was in his stomach a slow, cold, vast rising movement, as though he held within the embrace of his bowels the swing of planets through space. He was giddy. He caught hold of himself, focused his attention to write again.

The details of the ransom drop follow. The only part of the note he pronounces "good" comes to him from another text:

> Now, about the money. How much? Yes; make it ten thousand. *Get ten thousand in 5 and 10 bills and put it in a shoe box....* That's good. He had read that somewhere....

and tomorrow night ride your car up and down Michigan Avenue from 35th Street to 40th Street. That would make it hard for anybody to tell just where Bessie would be hiding. He wrote: *Blink your headlights some. When you see a light in a window blink three times throw the box in the snow and drive off. Do what this letter say.* Now, he would sign it. But how? It should be signed in some way that would throw them off the trail. Oh, yes! Sign it "Red." He printed, *Red.*

Like Richard Wright himself in 1940, Bigger is compelled to sign his writing "Red." Yet the note is signed "Black" as well: "*Do what this letter say.*" Hidden behind the letter's detour through communism is the unmistakable stylistic trace of its black authorship. Yet no one in the novel seems to be able to read it. In passing under the signature "Red," the text's blackness is precisely what goes unread. Bigger is in fact present at the scene of the letter's reception, but he remains unseen, "nobody."

> The door swung in violently. Bigger started in fright. Mr. Dalton came into the kitchen, his face ashy. He stared at Peggy and Peggy, holding a dish towel in her hand, stared at him. In Mr. Dalton's hand was the letter, opened.
> "What's the matter, Mr. Dalton?"
> "Who.... Where did.... Who gave you this?"
> "What?"
> "This *letter*."
> "Why, nobody. I got it from the door."
> "When?"
> "A few minutes ago. Anything wrong?"
> Mr. Dalton looked around the entire kitchen, not at anything in particular, but just round the entire stretch of four walls, his eyes wide and unseeing.

Like Poe's purloined letter, the identity of the author of the note remains invisible because the detectives do not know how to read what is plainly there before them. Behind the sentence *"Do what this letter say"* lies the possibility—and the invisibility—of a whole vernacular literature.

KENETH KINNAMON ON THE CRITICAL RECEPTION OF THE NOVEL

Still other deletions may have occurred to Wright independently or have been suggested by Aswell or others. At one point Max is considering the paradoxes of racism. A white chauffeur arriving with the drunken daughter of his employer, he argues, would have informed him of her condition, but racist treatment of Bigger "made him do the *very* thing we did not want." Max goes farther: "Or, am I wrong? Maybe we *wanted* him to do it! Maybe we would have had no chance or justification to stage attacks against hundreds of thousands of people if he had acted sanely and normally! Maybe we would have had to go to the expensive length of inventing theories to justify our attacks if we had treated him fairly!" Such implausible and involuted speculation justifies deletion, but the cumulative effect of cuts involving racial politics, like that of those concerning Bigger's sexuality, is to lower the stridency of Wright's message, to soften the characterization, perhaps even to dilute the theme. One can maintain plausibly that deletions enhanced the literary value of Book 3, or even that more cuts would have improved it further, but the fact remains that Wright finally decided or was persuaded to let Max say less than he said through the drafts and unrevised galleys. In the case of *Native Son*, Edward Aswell, a white liberal from Tennessee and Harvard who had been Thomas Wolfe's editor and was to become Wright's valued friend, may even be regarded as standing in relation to Wright as Max stands in relation to Bigger: sympathetic, loyal, analytical, understanding to a point, but not quite ready to accept the full and uncut expression of a sensibility so radically different from his own.

Moreover, Aswell decided at the last minute not to let *Native Son* go unmediated into the world. In early summer of 1939 the Book-of-the-Month Club had expressed interest in the novel. On 23 September his literary agent wrote Wright optimistically: "We have always understood that Dorothy Canfield has as much or more influence in the Book-of-the-Month Club than anyone else so I am really quite hopeful though I don't know anything about it." Fisher, a productive and well-known writer, was a member of the board of selection. The matter dragged on for the rest of the year, delaying publication by several months. Never before had the Book-of-the-Month Club selected a novel by a black writer. Finally, early in the new year, Aswell wrote with the good news that the book had been selected as a March alternate. Furthermore, he noted that "Dorothy Canfield Fisher has written a brief Introduction." Nine days later he expressed satisfaction with Fisher's effort and his regret that Wright had not had an opportunity to see it: "Under ordinary circumstances, if there had been more time, we should have wanted to consult you before deciding to put in it [sic]. Pressed as we were, I took the responsibility of saying that I felt pretty sure you would approve. I hope I have not guessed wrong." Presented with a fait accompli and the likelihood that the Book-of-the-Month Club would not accept the novel as a selection without the introduction, Wright could do little but assent with as much grace as he could muster. After another week Aswell wrote: "I am glad you liked Dorothy Canfield's Introduction."[33]

What we have here is a latter-day example of the process of white authentication that Robert Stepto has shown to be so characteristic a feature of slave narratives.[34] In this process a well-known white abolitionist would provide a preface, guarantee, or letter attesting to the veracity or historicity of the narrative and the genuineness of the author's credentials. Only with such a seal of approval, the feeling was, would a predominantly white audience be receptive to a black story. The difficulty was that the authenticator's white perspective inevitably distorted as it mediated the necessarily different black perspective of the author. Max and Bigger again—or Aswell and Wright.

Dorothy Canfield Fisher of Arlington, Vermont, was an influential and energetic white liberal with a steady stream of books to her credit since the first decade of the century. Nevertheless her credentials as a commentator on black life and letters were minimal: membership on the board of trustees of Howard University and treatment of a light family passing for white in the subplot of an early novel (*The Bent Twig*, 1915). But her most recent novel, *Seasoned Timber* (1939), was an attack on anti-Semitism. It must have seemed to Aswell that her heart was in the right place, and there could be little doubt that her endorsement would help sales. Her brief introduction is accurately characterized by Robert Stepto as "innocently vapid,"[35] but it is also confused, offering two opposed interpretations of Bigger. First, he is compared to a laboratory rat or sheep frustrated by the denial of fulfillment in American society. Then, as if to compensate for this emphasis on environmental determinism, she describes the theme of *Native Son* as "the Dostoievski subject—a human soul in hell because it is sick with a deadly spiritual sickness" (*NS*, x). She raises two points that many reviewers and readers seized upon, but she makes no effort to reconcile them. Steering the reader in advance in opposite directions, Fisher's introduction does the novel a disservice. Writing to Aswell several years later about a preface to *Black Boy* (the proposed title at the time was American Hunger), Wright commented: "I'm wondering if the reader himself will not make up his mind as to what I'm trying to do when he is wading into the book?"[36] The question is equally relevant to *Native Son*.

* * *

Wright's novel was born, then, with the assistance of various white midwives, male and female. However much domesticated by white assistance at its delivery, it was still a robust infant whose loud cries reverberated through the literary atmosphere as the 1940s began. By presenting Bigger as he was—"resentful toward whites, sullen, angry, ignorant, emotionally unstable, depressed and unaccountably elated at times, and unable even, because of his own lack of inner organization which American oppression has fostered in him, to unite with members of his own race"[37]—Wright knew that he risked confirming in white minds a racist stereotype, that his own comrades in the Communist party might reject his complex emotional and artistic honesty, and that the black bourgeoisie would be shamed by his frankness and would urge him to accentuate the positive in his racial portrayal. In a real sense, then, Wright was not so much appealing to his audiences as he was confronting them with a harsh and unpalatable truth, forcing them to undergo such emotional turmoil as to reexamine their attitudes and expand their awareness of the meaning, universally existential and politically revolutionary as well as racially revealing, of Bigger Thomas. Wright would assault his readers' sensibilities, not curry their favor or indulge their sentimentality.

How well did he succeed? If there is one common denominator to the 423 reviews, notices, essays, lectures, sermons, editorials, letters to the editor, and poems that appeared in the two years after the publication of the novel, it is their testimonial to the *power* of the work, the searing emotional force that gripped readers with or against their will. "Shock our sensibilities," "tremendous wallop," "power and drama and truth," "throbs from the opening line, with a wallop propelled to the end," "tremendous power," "a terrible story, a horrible story," "its frank brutalities ... will horrify many readers," "powerful story," "powerful novel," "engrossing, terrible story," "a supershocker," "grim and frightening," "one of the most powerful novels of all time"—such phrases recurred many scores of times in the reviews of *Native Son*.[38] So powerful was its impact that one reviewer could only describe it as "a book which takes you by the ears and gives you a good shaking, whirls you on your toes and slaps you dizzy against the wall."[39] When the reader regained full consciousness, one supposes, he or she could then ponder the message Wright had conveyed with such overpowering force.

Doing so, the reader was likely to note the thematic issues of race and politics and the literary qualities of narration and characterization. Whatever its universal dimensions, *Native Son* is first of all a novel about the American racial situation, and this aspect of its theme elicited comment from almost all of its reviewers. For most, regardless of race or region, Wright made a cogent as well as a moving case against white racism. As far north as Maine an anonymous reviewer noted that Bigger was a victim of environmental determinism: "a mean Negro who might have been a solid asset in another environment." As far south as Houston another claimed that "Wright makes a masterful, unrelenting appeal" for racial understanding, however much other Southerners may object to the novel's theme. In the Midwest a reviewer judged that "the picture of the Negro, against the white world, as presented by Wright, is the most illuminating I have ever read," and in California students emphasized its importance as a revelation of social injustice and a demand for change.[40]

Concerning the strictly literary qualities of the novel, discussion centered around narration and characterization, with only a few perceptive observers noting Wright's symbolism. A clear consensus of praise for the work's literary artistry emerged, even from many who objected to its themes. Repeatedly the driving narrative momentum with its strong dramatic quality was singled out for favorable comment: "for the first two-thirds of the book," an influential Midwestern reviewer wrote, "no tale of pursuit and capture has rivaled it."[41] Likewise Wright's characterization, especially of Bigger, was widely admired, many reviewers agreeing with Henry Seidel Canby's early comment that "only a Negro could have written" such a psychologically penetrating book.[42] Canby and a few others, indeed, seemed to emphasize the psychological dimension of Wright's story as a way of evading the social message. But more often reviewers considered characterization as well as narrative pace and structure as a means of realizing the author's theme. Many agreed with a reviewer in Albany, New York: "He has proven with this vigorous novel that for psychological imagination, for power of dramatic construction, for the convincingness and reality of his characters, he has few equals."[43] Reviewers who noted Wright's symbolism, his crisp dialogue, his "prose ... as firm as steel,"[44] and his satiric touches helped to amplify the artistic particulars of the craft that had produced such a powerful effect.

Notes

33. Aswell to Wright, 2 January, 11 January, 18 January 1940, Wright Archive.

34. Stepto, *From behind the Veil*, 3–31.

35. Ibid., 129.

36. Wright to Aswell, 14 January 1944, Box 34, Harper & Brothers Collection, Princeton University Library. Fisher was chosen instead of Wright to provide the introduction to *Black Boy* as well!

37. Wright, *How "Bigger" Was Born*, 21.

38. See "*Afro* Readers Write about 'Native Son'"; "Among Books Reviewed in March"; "Highlights in New Books"; "'Native Son' Delves Into Race Problems"; "Negro's Answer"; "A Remarkable Book by Negro"; "Wright, Richard" (*Booklist*); "Wright, Richard" (*Pratt Booklist*); "A Powerful Novel of Negro's Struggle in a White World"; Fairall, "An Engrossing, Terrible Story"; Gannett, "Books and Things"; Gray, "A Disturbing View"; "Another 'American Tragedy.'"

39. Davis, "Books of the Week in Review."

40. "Books and Bookfolk"; "Negro's Novel Is Overwhelming"; "Powerful Plea for Negro Race"; Ball, "The Vicarious World"; Dalton, "First Novel Wins Acclaim."

41. Butcher, "Negro Writes Brilliant Novel."

42. Canby, "*Native Son* by Richard Wright."

43. L[ewis], "Between the Book Covers."

44. Berry, "The World of Books."

JAMES NAGEL ON BLINDNESS AS A METAPHOR

As several critics have already pointed out,[2] the central image in its various forms is that of blindness. Literally, blindness relates only to Mrs. Dalton, who is in fact without sight and whose disability permits and provokes the murder of her daughter. She is also blind, however, in a figurative sense (as are all the rest of the characters) in that she has virtually no insight into the realities of Negro life in Chicago. Like her husband, she sees Bigger only as a type, a generalized object of her cathartic altruism that is expected to respond to generosity with gratitude and humility but not with any overt expressions of individualism. Thus she is blind on two counts, a condition symbolic of the depth of the "blindness of the white liberal philanthropic community,"[3] as Edward Margolies has pointed out.

But Mrs. Dalton is not the only character whose vision and understanding have been impaired. Britten, for example, sees only "communists" and "niggers." To Dalton he says: "Well, you see 'em one way and I see 'em another. To me, a nigger's a nigger" (p. 154). It should be also noted that his attitude has been carefully foreshadowed by the frequent references to the peculiarities of his eyes (see pp. 146–53), beginning with Bigger's first exposure to him:

> The white man at Mr. Dalton's side [Britten] was squinting at him; he felt that tight, hot, choking fear returning. The white man clicked on the light. He had a cold, impersonal manner that told Bigger to be on his guard. In the very look of the man's eyes Bigger saw his own personality reflected in narrow, restricted terms. (p. 146)

And Bigger's first view of Britten is no better. He sees Mr. Dalton and the investigator only in "red darkness" and as "white discs of danger" (p. 146). To Bigger he is an enemy and easily recognizable: "Britten was familiar to him; he had met a thousand Brittens in his life" (p. 154). Thus both of them are reduced to a "type" in the eyes of the other.[4]

In fact, until the first murder Bigger is as blind as anyone: he does not understand himself and plays no clear role in either his family, gang, or society. Those around him are equally sightless: Bessie, for example, is twice mentioned as being blind (pp. 132, 165) as is Reverend Hammond, who casts his gaze on a more promising vision of the promised land.

At one point he asks Bigger to "Fergit yuh's black" (p. 263). Indeed, in Bigger's mind, at least, nearly everyone is blind: "His feet were cold and he stamped them in the snow, surrounded by people waiting, too, for a car. He did not look at them; they were simply blind people, blind like his mother, his brother, his sister, Peggy, Britten, Jan, Mr. Dalton, and the sightless Mrs. Dalton and the quiet empty houses with their black gaping windows."[5] (pp. 163–64).

Perhaps Bigger's inability to see and understand the world about him precludes the possibility of his realizing that anyone is more insightful than he.[6] In some respects he is right: the newspapers reduce him to a dehumanized "ape" and the police underestimate him to the extent of suspecting an accomplice on the grounds that "the plan of the murder and kidnapping was too elaborate to be the work of a Negro mind" (p. 229). Apparently they have not "seen" him at all, a fact he senses in counting on their blindness for his escape.

Thus blindness is operative throughout the novel as a metaphor of a lack of understanding and of a tendency to generalize individuals on the basis of race. It is both a rationalization for those who are looking and a disguise for those who are being looked at. This concept is expressed in other terms as well: Wright continually refers to a "curtain" or "barrier" which prevents his characters from fully seeing and communicating with others, particularly those of another race. Because of it, Bigger is alienated from even his friends and isolated behind his symbolic "curtain." Threatened by the shame of acknowledging the living conditions of his family, he erects a protective barrier: "he lived with them, but behind a wall, a curtain" (p. 14); and, again: "All that morning he had lurked behind his curtain of indifference and looked at things, snapping and glaring at whatever had tried to make him come out into the open" (p. 31).

Sometimes the "wall" seems the result of a deterministic force which prevents him from establishing rapport with anyone. Jan, for example, tries to reach Bigger on the street after being questioned at the Daltons', but despite his intentions, circumstances prevent full communication: "In the pale yellow sheen of the street lamp they faced each other; huge wet flakes of snow floated down slowly, forming a delicate screen between them" (pp. 161–62).

Throughout *Native Son* this metaphor is reminiscent of the "veil" concept explored in *The Souls of Black Folk*,[7] by W. E. Burghardt DuBois. DuBois, of course, was writing much earlier (1903), but the meaning of the device is, tragically, much the same. The veil, he points out, not only prevents whites and blacks from seeing each other, but also deters a Negro from truly seeing himself: "After the Egyptian and Indian, the Greek and Roman, the Negro is a sort of seventh son, born with a veil, and gifted with a second-sight in this American world—a world which yields him no true self-consciousness, but only lets him see himself through the revelation of the other world" (DuBois, p. 16).

The result is an imposed self-destruction of identity, with the white-ideal constantly at odds with the reality of blackness. This dichotomy, DuBois suggests, promotes a unique duality, perpetually schizophrenic, in one's view of himself: "It is a peculiar sensation, this double-consciousness, this sense of always looking at one's self through the eyes of others, of measuring one's soul by the tape of a world that looks on in amused contempt and pity. One ever feels his two-ness—an American, a Negro; two souls, two thoughts, two unreconciled strivings; two warring ideals in one dark body, whose dogged strength alone keeps it from being torn asunder" (DuBois, pp. 16–17).

Thus the veil, like blindness, creates a sense of isolation within impregnable walls and transfers a pathological dualism from society to the oppressed individual.

What DuBois is talking about seems very close to the situation Bigger finds himself in:

> But what was he after? What did he want? What did he love and what did he hate? He did not know. There was something he *knew* and something he *felt*; something the world gave him and something he *himself* had; something spread out in *front* of him and something spread out in *back*: and never in all his life, with this black skin of his, had the two worlds, thought and feeling, will and mind, aspiration and satisfaction, been together; never had he felt a sense of wholeness (p. 225)

Notes

2. See, for example, Robert A. Bone, *The Negro Novel in America* (New Haven, 1968), pp. 140–52, and Edward Margolies, "Richard Wright: *Native Son* and Three Kinds of Revolution," *Native Sons: A Critical Study of Twentieth-Century Negro American Authors* (New York, 1969), pp. 65–86.

3. Margolies, p. 84.

4. In addition, although the reader grows to know Bigger intimately, Britten remains stereotypic, the effect of which is to artistically restrict the vision of the reader. Thus he too becomes, very subtly, a participant in the blindness.

5. On another occasion he sees the windows of the empty building as the "eye-sockets of empty skulls" (p. 216).

6. Bigger's fear of and resistance to the white world is frequently symbolized by his gesture of throwing his hands up in front of his face. Generally this action occurs when he is attempting to blot out some detail which does not conform to his understanding of reality. For examples, see pp. 49–50, 95, 109, 133, 236, and 307.

7. W. E. Burghardt DuBois, *The Souls of Black Folk* (A Fawcett Premier Book: Greenwich, Conn., 1967).

ROSS PUDALOFF ON BIGGER'S APPETITES

An even more significant aspect of mass culture's influence upon Bigger occurs after Mary's death, at a time when he appears so fearful that he cannot shake down the ashes of the furnace where he disposed of her body. Bigger repeatedly desires to read the newspaper stories about the presumed disappearance of his victim. He has previously taken no interest in newspapers, with the possible exception that he may have used them to research the details of the ransom note which "he had read ... somewhere." With the intrusion of the reporters into the Daltons' basement, however, Bigger's interest in the publicity generated by his exploits assumes overwhelming importance in his life. When he sees the newspaper on the floor of the basement, his only wish is to read, even though Mary's body is still in the furnace. As he reads it, the reality of the story, which lists her as missing or kidnapped, is persuasive, even though he knows better: "It seems impossible that she was there in the fire, burning" if indeed the paper states otherwise.

Bigger continues to seek his identity in the newspapers even as his destiny grows progressively bleaker throughout the rest of the book. He wants to read "the story, his story" in the papers, and with this pun Wright collapses history into the contents of the front page to suggest that Bigger can understand himself only as a product of mass culture at its most destructive. Bigger searches for that "fullness" which he finds not in reality so much as in the representations of reality he encounters "when he read the newspapers or magazines, went to the movies, or walked along the streets with crowds...." Accordingly, he seeks "to lose himself in it so he could find himself," but the self he finds can only be found in those images of himself that the culture presents to him.

So important is this search for an identity that Bigger devises elaborate strategies to steal a paper in order to read about himself. Yet more revealing is his decision to risk exposure by leaving his hiding place to spend his last two cents on a newspaper. Even after his capture, Bigger desires to read what the papers are saying about him. So, after he has fainted at the coroner's inquest, he awakes in his cell physically and psychologically hungry. He appeases his appetites by first eating a meal with great relish, the first since his capture, and then asking the guard for a newspaper. It can be no accident that these two forms of consumption are linked in the text. What gives Bigger the ability to live and assert himself in the world is the act of consuming what the world gives him.[24]

Bigger's hunger after the coroner's inquest emphasizes the importance of consumption in a novel where many of the critical episodes occur during, or because of, eating and drinking. What is more, Bigger's initial response to his arrest had been to refuse to eat; his refusal can be understood as an attempt to establish a separate identity outside the power of mass culture. The scene in his prison cell also provides a perspective on Wright's use of documentary material in his fiction, what is sometimes called his "naturalism." The source for this scene is almost certainly the *Chicago Tribune*'s stories about Robert Nixon, whose murder case Wright followed from its beginning to Nixon's execution. According to the

Tribune, Nixon showed animation only "when he spoke of food" and "when he told of having been in the movies."[25] When Wright seized upon these seemingly dehumanizing and gratuitous details to compose his protagonist, he was not simply correcting the *Tribune*'s racism. He used them to explore the unsettling relationship between consumption and identity which they suggested to him. In 1948, Wright openly discussed the profoundly disturbing implications of consumption in mass society. Believing that it obliterated the basis for conventional political distinctions, he wrote, "The Right and Left, in different ways, have decided that man is a kind of animal whose needs can be met by making more and more articles for him to consume."[26]

Even though Bigger ultimately rejects the newspapers on grounds that they print "the same thing over and over again," his rejection of the overt aspects of mass culture does not mean he can reject that self that has derived from the media. Much of Bigger's character is best understood as having its origin in that popular figure of thirties melodrama, the tough guy. After Mary's body is discovered in the furnace, for example, Bigger reaches for his gun, thinking to himself "he would shoot before he would let them take him; it meant death either way, and he would die shooting every slug he had." Since this fantasy does not materialize, it prompts the reader to ask where the gratuitous lines come from and what function they serve in the novel. They obviously come from gangster movies and detective stories to shape Bigger's character; he has become what he has consumed. His attitudes about Bessie similarly mimic those of the hard-boiled school when he thinks to himself, "a woman was a dangerous burden when a man was running away." Furthermore, Wright locates the source of this notion of sex in what Bigger "had read of how men had been caught because of women." Most disastrously for Bessie, his decision to kill her comes as much from such American myths of sex, crime, and punishment as it does from any real danger she poses to him. Bigger knows that "some cold logic not his own, over which he had no control" demands her death. This explanation of his decision speaks to an otherwise controversial aspect of the text, for Bigger is under no other immediate necessity to kill Bessie, whom, paradoxically, he has forced to accompany him.[27]

Notes

24. In fact, hunger and eating are almost always given metaphoric and thematic significance by Wright. His original title for the autobiography was *American Hunger*, in many ways a more apt and revealing title than *Black Boy*. An interesting example of Wright's use of consumption is found in *Lawd Today*. Jake finds himself "hungering for more" as he dances with Blanche, a prostitute. The music promises him "an unattainable satisfaction." But what it provides is a particularly pernicious example of mass culture; the band plays "Is It True What They Say About Dixie," a lie Jake consumes and which consumes him. To further underline the damage done by mass culture, Jake and Blanche's verbal response to the music reveals a meaning of which they remain unaware: "'That's murder, Papa.' 'I want to be electrocuted,' he said" (*Lawd Today*, p. 207).

25. *Chicago Daily Tribune* (June 5, 1938), p. 6. There can be no doubt that Wright saw this story as he quoted other parts of it almost word for word, especially in the description of Bigger in *Native Son*. There was, of course, a more reasonable explanation of Nixon's interest in food provided by the *Chicago Defender* (June 18, 1938), p. 2. According to Robert Nixon, "they gave us that after they had whipped and kicked us and made us confess."

26. Quoted in Fabre, *The Unfinished Quest*, p. 325.

27. For example, Addison Gayle finds Bessie's murder "the weakest incident in the novel" because it violates the black nationalism he sees as the basic thrust of the novel (*The Way of the New World: The Black Novel in America* [Garden City: Doubleday, 1975], p. 171). Perhaps the strongest defense of Bessie's murder is made by Donald B. Gibson, "Richard Wright and the Tyranny of Convention," *CLAJ*, 12 (June, 1969), 349. He argues that Bigger kills Bessie so as to be "emotionally convinced that he has murdered Mary, for he projects the consciousness of the later act back into the former." But even such an explanation does not fully answer the question of the origin of Bigger's motives, for Gibson does not argue that Bigger is aware of these reasons. One significant change in the dramatized version of *Native Son* was the manner and cause of Bessie's (renamed Clara in the play) death. After she has accidentally led the police to Bigger's hideout, he grows angry with her, threatens to kill her, and does hit her. But when the police start to shoot, Bigger is "holding Clara protectively in front of him" and she is killed by a police bullet (Paul Green and Richard Wright, *Native Son (The Biography of a Young*

American): A Play in Ten Scenes [New York: Harper and Brothers, 1941], pp. 119–20). Such a change gains sympathy for Bigger by making him the victim rather than the villain of melodrama.

JAMES SMETHURST ON WRIGHT'S USE OF DOUBLING

The gothic also mystifies the social system in other ways, most notably through a type of transference. Thus we see a sort of doubling in which an African American character, generally Bigger, becomes a double or stand-in for a white character, allowing the black character unconsciously to reenact and control a formerly uncontrollable situation. For example, Bigger, psychologically unable to rob the white storekeeper Blum, recasts his fellow gang member Gus as Blum and beats up, and symbolically rapes, Gus. Likewise, Bessie becomes a double of Mary Dalton in that her rape by Bigger is actual and her murder intentional, whereas the rape of Mary was a half-formed desire and her murder accidental. Other moments of black–white doubling include the pairing of Bigger's brother Buddy with the young white Communist Jan Erlone, Mrs. Thomas with the Dalton's Irish servant Peggy, and in a very telling scene the doubling lifestyles of the rich and famous in the film *The Gay Woman* with a stereotypically savage Africa in *Trader Horn*, which Jack and Bigger watch in a double feature. And, of course, there is the opening moment of terrifying and uncanny doubling in which Bigger kills a version of himself: a monstrous black rat filled with rage and fear.

A similar sort of doubling also takes place in which Bigger posits two Biggers—one who is in control of himself and one who is controlled by gothic terror: "There were two Biggers: one was determined to get rest and sleep at any cost; and the other shrank from images charged with terror" (237). In much the same way Bigger also sees two bizarrely dissociated Bessies—a corporeal Bessie entirely under his control and a consciousness who contests that control and demands things of him: "As he walked beside her he felt that there were two Bessies: one a body that he had just had and wanted badly again; and the other was in Bessie's face; it asked questions; it bargained and sold the other to best advantage" (233).

Both of these doublings—the pairing of black and white and the bifurcation of the individual—are aspects of a sort of gothic vision by which Bigger attempts to interpret and control his environment. Or at least these doublings allow Bigger to control himself enough to be able to act in some manner which validates him as a person—at least in his own view—within that environment. Needless to say, this vision is severely distorted, not to say psychotic.

Though this doubling or identification between apparently disparate people and things allows Bigger at least an imagined control of his situation, there is another side to this projection. This side is the further mystification of the social system when uncontrollable or inescapable elements of that system are projected onto various objects. There is a constant reference to the whiteness of things that Bigger sees: walls, smoke, clouds, snow, cigarettes, hair, and so on. This white hems Bigger in just as violence, real estate covenants, gentlemen's agreements, and so on hem in Chicago's African Americans behind the veil of the South Side "Black Belt."

Perhaps the most notable example of this projection is onto the Dalton's white cat, an obvious intertextual allusion to Poe's "The Black Cat," in which the Dalton's cat embodies the white supervision of the black subject. This sense of being watched might be displaced onto a weird object by Bigger, but it could hardly be called paranoid since the reader gets to see the whole machinery of supervision—the police, the press, the state's attorney, the detective, and various other witnesses and experts as well as the self-supervision which has been ideologically induced largely by mass culture in Bigger—in some detail. (In this regard, the projection of white supervision onto the cat is the flip side, so to speak, of the projection of a certain black self-policing onto the black rat from the novel's opening.) But to say that Bigger's vision, or narrative if you will, is not paranoid does not mean that this projection, though emotionally or psychologically powerful, helps him understand how the system works. Quite the contrary, it makes such an understanding impossible. In short, while the virtual blizzard of whiteness is a powerful metaphor for a system of supervision and control and its effect on the black subject, what is required is the examination and understanding of that system through some scientific method, say dialectical materialism, not simply a representation of that system.

Again, it should be noted that such mystification and misunderstanding are not restricted to Bigger. They are characteristic of virtually everyone the reader encounters in *Native Son*. Once again Wright utilizes a central gothic convention, a terror of incomprehension. This is the terror that the world one inhabits is guided by rules other than those one is able to see, or that within one's world or very close to it are contained secrets—deeds, other selves, sisters, explanations—of crucial importance to us if only one could find them.

CRAIG WERNER ON BIGGER'S BLUES

The murders of Mary and Bessie bring this long-standing sense of dislocation to a climax. Bigger senses that his violence is inextricably linked to the city in which he lives; each murder is accompanied by a redefinition of Bigger's sense of what the city means. Immediately after realizing that Mary is dead, Bigger experiences the city—imaged as a totally white presence—as an absolute determinant of his actions: "The reality of the room fell from him; the vast city of white people that sprawled outside took its place" (p. 75 [86]). Having crossed the threshold into the metaphysical darkness of the ornate old building, however, his sense of the city undergoes a profound transformation. Immediately before he kills Bessie, he experiences a moment in which "the city did not exist" (p. 199 [221]). Torn between these extremes—experiencing a tension of a sort basic to the modernist sensibility—Bigger gradually realizes that the question is not whether or not the city exists; rather it is what his own consciousness *makes* of the city. Associating the city with the whiteness of the fallen snow, Bigger—like many modernist criminal-artist-metaphysical picaros—begins to explore his own sense-making process: "The snow had stopped falling and the city, white, still, was a vast stretch of roof-tops and sky. He had been thinking about it for hours here in the dark and now there it was, all white, still. But what he had thought about it had made it real with a reality it did not have now in the daylight. When lying in the dark thinking of it, it seemed to have something which left it when it was looked at" (p. 204 [226]).

This ever-changing waste land exerts a profoundly fragmenting impact on Bigger's consciousness. In *How "Bigger" Was Born*, Wright echoes DuBois's analysis of double consciousness when he traces the Afro-American sense of fragmentation to the existence of "two worlds, the white world and the black world." The split is as much psychological as political, because "the very tissue of [Afro-Americans'] consciousness received its tone and timbre from the strivings of that dominant civilization." Aggravating the racially specific problem for Bigger is the fact that even the dominant civilization had come to perceive itself as a waste land. Wright observes that Bigger is a "product of a dislocated society; he is a dispossessed and disinherited man; he is all of this, and he lives amid the greatest possible plenty on earth and he is looking and feeling for a way out."[20] Although Wright pursues the implications of this observation in specifically political terms, the description would serve as well for Eliot's J. Alfred Prufrock. Like his modernist contemporaries, Bigger experiences a profound sense of entrapment emanating from a confusion of subjective and objective that subverts his sense of self. Just as the city assumes an organic quality, other people repeatedly lose their human solidity, casting Bigger adrift in a world of semianimate barriers. Mary and Jan seem "two vast white looming walls" (p. 59 [68]). When he is captured, Bigger looks out at "a circle of white faces; but he was outside of them, behind his curtain, his wall" (p. 228 [252]). In this context, the similarity between the modernist malaise and DuBoisian double consciousness seems clear. Both alienate the individual from any unified sensibility. Throughout

Native Son, Bigger feels his own fragmentation: "He was divided and pulled against himself" (p. 21 [27]); "There were two Biggers" (p. 214 [236–7]). Such division seems the inevitable response to a context in which every word, every symbol possesses at least two—and frequently many more— possible meanings. The cross of the preachers and the cross of the Ku Klux Klan dissolve into one another in Bigger's fragmented consciousness (p. 287 [313]). Although he lacks words to express his sense of this fragmentation—and in this he is as much modernist artist/hero as the inarticulate victim described by Ellison—Bigger is acutely aware of his own lack of wholeness: "never in all his life, with this black skin of his, had the two worlds, thought and feeling, will and mind, aspiration and satisfaction, been together; never had he felt a sense of wholeness" (pp. 203–4 [225]). As he prepares for death, Bigger's apprehension of his fragmentation takes the form of an intensely solipsistic speculation which would not be out of place in a Beckett mindscape: "If he were nothing, if this were all, then why could not he die without hesitancy? Who and what was he to feel the agony of a wonder so intensely that it amounted to fear? Why was this strange impulse always throbbing in him when there was nothing outside of him to meet it and explain it? Who or what had traced this restless design in him? Why was this eternal reaching for something that was not there? Why this black gulf between him and the world: warm red blood here and cold blue sky there, and never a wholeness, a oneness, a meeting of the two?" (p. 350–1 [383]).

Bigger's internal response to his fragmentation, like those of "metaphysical picaros" from Leopold Bloom to Tyrone Slothrop of *Gravity's Rainbow*, passes through several distinct phases. Gradually, Bigger's initial disorientation gives way to an exhilarating sense of himself as questing hero, which in turn disintegrates into a solipsistic sense of total meaninglessness, differing from the original situation because previously Bigger had been unaware of even the possibility of meaning. The final stage of Bigger's metaphysical wandering, explicitly recalling Eliot's "The Love Song of J. Alfred Prufrock," involves a direct confrontation with the association of criminal and artist in the modernist sensibility, an extended meditation on what it means "to murder and create."

At the outset of *Native Son*, Bigger embodies, to use Wright's phrase from *How "Bigger" Was Born*, "a hot and whirling vortex of undisciplined and unchannelized impulses."[21] His perception oscillates wildly between extreme subjectivity and extreme objectivity: "The sharp precision of the world of steel and stone dissolved into blurred waves. He blinked and the world grew hard again, mechanical, distinct" (p. 14 [19]). Similar feelings of being cast adrift in a discontinuous world recur throughout the novel. Confronting the journalists in the Dalton basement, Bigger feels that "Events were like the details of a tortured dream, happening without cause. At times it seemed that he could not quite remember what had gone before and what it was he was expecting to come" (p. 169 [187]). Paralyzed by this Dostoevskian "deadlock of impulses" which renders him "unable to rise to the land of the living" (p. 83 [93]), Bigger experiences himself as a cipher, surrendering all sense of control to the mechanical world around him: "He was not driving; he was simply sitting and floating along smoothly through darkness" (p. 67 [77–8]).

This feeling of ease, of course, collapses almost immediately, leaving Bigger with only the darkness. His growing awareness of alienation, however, marks the beginning of a significant new stage of Bigger's metaphysical journey. Whereas in the "Fear" section Bigger seems unaware of the relationship between external and internal experience, in "Flight" he senses the importance of sense-making processes to the construction of reality. This recognition begins as a vague desire to resist being defined by the discourses which surround him. In a sequence of passages recalling Pound's imagist principle of "Direct presentation of the 'thing,' whether subjective or objective," Bigger "wished that he could be an idea in their minds" (p. 110 [123]). At several points, he immerses himself directly in a level of experience which strips away the verbal discourse—the Eliotic "babble of voices" (p. 184 [204])—that surrounds him: "The world of sound fell abruptly away from him and a vast picture appeared before his eyes, a picture teeming with so much meaning that he could not react to it all at once" (p. 116 [129–30]). Bigger enters this new realm of experience with a feeling of exhilaration grounded on an unfamiliar sense of his own significance: "he held within the embrace of his bowels the swing of planets through space" (p. 151 [167]).

This sense of liberation from external discourses, however, generates its own countermovement, plunging Bigger into solipsistic isolation. An extreme, and dangerous, separation from the external social realities that condition his consciousness accompanies Bigger's growing awareness of the world of images: "He had been so deeply taken up with his own thoughts that he did not know if he had actually heard anything or had imagined it" (p. 162 [179]). As the external forces reassert their power, Bigger struggles to maintain a grasp on his internal reality, which Wright images increasingly in terms of total isolation. Staring into the airshaft of the old ornate building, Bigger projects his sense of desolation: "He looked downward and saw nothing but black darkness into which now and then a few flakes of white floated from the sky" (p. 196 [217]). Again, the description suggests Beckett. Echoing the Faulkner of *The Sound and the Fury*, Wright associates this landscape with Bigger's experience of a meaninglessness which he feels all the more intensely for his dawning sense of his own significance: "Outside in the cold night the wind moaned and died down, like an idiot in an icy black pit" (p. 200 [221]).

Notes

20. Wright, *How "Bigger" Was Born*, pp. 7, 8, 19.
21. Ibid., p. 18.

Yoshinobu Hakutani on *Native Son* and American Culture

To present a sociological observation based on determinism, Wright uses in *Native Son* a variety of devices quite different from those in *Pudd'nhead Wilson*. There is a clear distinction, first of all, between the motives of the two novelists. Twain, a liberal thinker, wrote out of deep sympathy for the racially oppressed, and the fault he had to avoid was sentimentality. Wilson, neither the oppressor nor the oppressed, can take a neutral stand. Not only does Twain's point of view sound scientific and impersonal, but it is conveyed with humor and seldom turns into pity. Wright, on the other hand, was motivated by wrongs he had personally suffered, and his vision had no room for humor or levity. Unlike *Pudd'nhead Wilson*, *Native Son* from the first page keeps the reader vividly aware of the protagonist as the inevitable product of his environment. As the story unfolds, this portrait is gradually intensified with the events that follow his capture. The lurid trial and Bigger's defense by a radical attorney enable *Native Son* to express the whole tragedy of black people rather than one individual's pathology.

Wright's most effective technique in *Native Son* as a racial discourse is the conversion of Max's speech into a narrative voice, which in turn coordinates the findings of a sociological analysis with Bigger's personal grievances. Such a voice triumphantly counteracts the travesty that is the state's case. Unable to support his claim with factual evidence or rudimentary logic, the prosecutor piles up statements of racial prejudice and hatred reminiscent of those of Ku Klux Klansmen. Those who regard Max's speech as didactic and uninspiring are surprised at Bigger's intellectual growth at the end of the trial. The views Bigger expresses toward the end of his life become abstract; earlier he has been compelled to act by his social environment, but through Max's speech he begins to establish his own identity. As a result, he is able to conceptualize the meaning of his act and is proud of his manhood and independence. What he achieves at the end of his life, despite the death sentence, thus contributes to Wright's thematic design.

Max's role in pleading for Bigger, then, differs from Wilson's in identifying the murderer. Max, being Jewish, has a deeper understanding of the conflict of races in America than does Wilson. Wilson, characterized as absentminded, keeps himself out of the racial strife in the local community. One can only speculate why Wright deleted in the 1940 Harper edition of *Native Son* a reference to Max's being a Jew, but because Wright's intention was to indict American society, he made Max's speech reflect a racially impersonal point of view. In the manuscript version of *Native Son*, Max states: "And, because I, a Jew, dared defend this Negro boy, for days my mail has been flooded with threats against my life. The manner in which Bigger Thomas was captured, the hundreds of innocent Negro homes invaded, the scores of Negroes assaulted upon the streets, the dozens who were thrown out of their jobs, the barrage of lies poured out from every source against a defenseless people—all of this was something unheard of in democratic lands" (*EW*, 806). This passage was deleted in the Harper edition. Max's observations on Bigger's condition in America strike the literary public, not the courtroom audience, as eminently true and brilliant. The objectivity in Max's vision therefore contrasts sharply but finely with the bigotry in the prosecutor's probing.

Despite the obvious difference in the roles Max and Wilson assume, the visions their speeches create are both ironic. As Wilson tells the court that Tom is an innocent victim instead of a murderer, Max testifies that society instead of Bigger is a murderer. Even the well-meaning Daltons—like Judge Driscoll, "respected, esteemed, and beloved by all the community," and who considers himself a "free-thinker" (*PW*, 4)—are depicted as prejudiced and condescending. Although they appear philanthropic since they donate money for black boys to buy ping-pong tables, they are in fact exploiters of the poor and disadvantaged. At the coroner's inquest Max questions Mr. Dalton with sarcasm: "So, the profits you take from the Thomas family in rents, you give back to them to ease the pain of their gouged lives and to salve the ache of your own conscience?" (*NS*, 304). As Benjamin Davis Jr. pointed out in his review of *Native Son*, Dalton's philanthropy as Max satirizes it resembles that of "the class of hypocritical Carnegies, Fords and Rockefellers, who are the very causes of the unemployment, poverty and misery among the Negro people, which their million-dollar gifts are falsely alleged to cure."[23] Theodore Dreiser as a young reporter in Pittsburgh in the mid-1890s witnessed such hypocrisy in Andrew Carnegie. In his magazine articles and later in his autobiography, *A Book about Myself*, Dreiser satirized Carnegie's appearance of generosity in contributing part of his huge fortunes to various libraries. In reality, Dreiser subtly noted, Carnegie was an exploiter of cheap labor in Pittsburgh, an egocentric public figure. "Selfish wealth," Dreiser remarked with a bit of sarcasm, "stands surprised, amazed, almost indignant, at the announcement that Andrew Carnegie, instead of resting in Olympian luxury on the millions he has earned, and going to the grave with his gold tightly clutched in his stiffening fingers, proposes to expend the bulk of his riches, during his lifetime, for the benefit of his fellowmen."[24]

Max's final speech in the court also abounds in irony. While Max is aware of the racist tone of the press against Bigger, he deplores "the silence of the church." "What is the cause of all this high feeling and excitement?" he asks. "Is it the crime of Bigger Thomas? Were Negroes liked yesterday and hated today because of what he has done?" Indicting the judicial system, Max says: "Gangsters have killed and have gone free to kill again. But none of that brought forth an indignation to equal this" (*NS*, 356). Personally as well, Max satirizes the landlord Dalton who refuses to rent apartments to black people anywhere but in the Black Belt. According to Max, then, it turns out that confining Bigger "in that forest" as a stranger had in fact made him an acquaintance of Mary, whom he murdered. And to Mrs. Dalton, Max ironically says: "Your philanthropy was as tragically blind as your sightless eyes!" (*NS*, 362). Through his killing of a white girl, Bigger is able to see himself as an individual. As James Nagel points out, this scene becomes "the pivotal point for not only the structure and theme but the imagery as well: it is a moment of 'recognition' in the classical sense."[25]

Notes
23. Review from *Sunday Worker*, in Reilly, 70.
24. "A Monarch of Metal Workers—Andrew Carnegie."
25. "Images of 'Vision,'" 113.

JOYCE ANN JOYCE ON WRIGHT'S USE OF THE WORD BLACK

Wright's ingenious use of periodic, balanced, and compound sentences is only part of the intricate language system through which Bigger's tragic fate evolves. Complementing Bigger's ambiguous characterization and the ironic events that shape his destiny are the interconnections among the rhythmic sentence patterns; the colors black, white, and yellow; the images of the wall, the sun, and the snow; and the metaphor of blindness. In their figurative function, the wall and the color black unite with the balanced sentence in their portrayal of Bigger's helplessness and physical impotence. Suggestive of the entrapment described in the balanced sentence, black represents the fear and humiliation Bigger feels in the face of the white world. Upon Bigger's initial visit to the Dalton home, the fear and shame he feels in the presence of whites are so intense that he remains on the verge of hysteria during the entire interview with Mr. Dalton. Thus when Bigger first meets Mr. Dalton, the word *black* accentuates the psychological chasm that separates the two men: "Grabbing the arms of the chair, he pulled himself upright and found a tall, lean, white-haired man holding a piece of paper in his hand. The man was gazing at him with an amused smile that made him conscious of every square inch of skin on his *black* body" (39, emphasis mine). Mr. Dalton's "amused smile" reflects the superiority, power, and emotional distance characteristic of a representative from the godlike world that controls Bigger's life. It is no accident that this white-haired man holds a (white) piece of paper. These symbols are markers for the subjugation that causes Bigger to recoil in acute awareness of his blackness. Consequently,

Wright's use of *black* interacts with setting. For just as Mr. Dalton is identified with the power and stability cultivated by his environment, Bigger's encounter with that environment produces feelings of inferiority and entrapment.

Although the word *black* appears throughout the novel, two other passages make especially vivid its metaphorical dimensions. The first occurs in the scene in which Bigger murders Bessie. Despite the fact that Bessie coerces Bigger into confiding in her, once she learns of the magnitude of his crime she desperately wants to retreat. Bigger must then keep her with him until he realizes that her extreme fear will only accelerate his capture. Soon after he decides that he has to kill her, they step into a deserted building to rest. Wright uses *black* three times in this single passage to underscore Bessie's despair and impotence:

> He [Bigger] put his shoulder to it [the door] and gave a stout shove; it yielded grudgingly. It was *black* inside and the feeble glow of the flashlight did not help much.... He circled the spot of the flashlight; the floor was carpeted with *black* dirt and he saw two bricks lying in corners. He looked at Bessie; her hands covered her face and he could see the damp of tears on her *black* fingers. (196, emphasis mine)

Black in this passage connects with Wright's use of setting to reflect Bigger's growing feelings of entrapment and fear. It also suggests that Bessie's cowering and feelings of remorse stem from her humiliation at her blackness as well as her fear of the white world.

The other scene in which *black* is used with especially strong significance occurs during Rev. Hammond's visit with Bigger in jail in Book 3. Rev. Hammond epitomizes the Black community's acceptance of the guilt and shame that arise from their blackness. Bigger intuitively associates the newspapers' descriptions of him as brutish, ignorant, and inferior with Rev. Hammond's passivity and penitence:

He [Bigger] stared at the man's jet-black suit and remembered who he was.... And at once he was on guard against the man.... He feared that the preacher would make him feel remorseful. He wanted to tell him to go; but so closely associated in his mind was the man with his mother and what she stood for that he could not speak. In his feelings he could not tell the difference between what this man evoked in him and what he read in the papers.... (240, emphasis mine)

Here *black* is the touchstone for Bigger's response to Rev. Hammond, his Job-like rejection of this counselor's religious palaver. The use of the word *black* appears to be inadvertent in the one-line paragraph after Rev. Hammond's prayer for Bigger: "Bigger's black face rested in his hands and he did not move" (243). Actually, *black* functions here as the symbolic finale of the suffering, shame, and penitence expressed in the prayer. When Bigger eventually pulls the preacher's cross from around his neck, he demonstrates his final rejection of the humiliation linked to his blackness.

A traditional metaphor for impotence and resistance (Cirlot 343), the image of the wall accompanies *black* and Wright's use of setting to reflect his character's state of mind by representing limiting situations or obstructions that challenge Bigger. Wright's rhythmic use of the image of the wall satisfies T. R. Henn's description of what he refers to as dominant images in his discussion of those characteristic of the tragic structure. A dominant image is "one or more images that, by specific statement or inference, provide a framework or theme for the play; and in terms of which part or all of the dramatic statement is made. These will be of varying degrees of subtlety ..." (135). Of more than twenty-nine instances in which Wright depicts Bigger or Bessie physically backed against a wall, the two most powerful scenes, filled with persistent references to wall, both take place in the basement of the Dalton home.

In both scenes the basement and the furnace containing Mary's burning body unite as the focus of the ultimate tests that confront Wright's hero. In addition to the fact that the basement becomes the gathering place for the newspaper reporters and Britten, Mr. Dalton's private detective, the droning furnace also serves as a constant reminder of Bigger's vulnerability. Dominating these scenes, the walls of the basement surrounding Bigger emphasize the extent of his entrapment and the severity of his physical impotence. After he has burned Mary's body and chosen to remain in the Dalton home, his first major challenge is to withstand Britten's hostility and to delude him as he has the Daltons. As Britten questions him, Bigger ponders on the furnace: "The fire sang in Bigger's ears and he saw the red shadows dance on the walls" (133). The more Britten confronts Bigger, the more Bigger thinks of the furnace and meets Britten's challenges with his mask of pusillanimity. When Britten finally thinks he has successfully identified Bigger as a Communist, the wall exemplifies the threatening power of the white world and Bigger's concomitant physical helplessness: "Britten followed Bigger till Bigger's head struck the wall. Bigger looked squarely into his eyes. Britten, with a movement so fast that Bigger did not see it, grabbed him in the collar and rammed his head hard against the wall" (137). Literally backing Bigger up against the wall, Britten, like a god, epitomizes the insensitivity and overwhelming authority of the white world.

Works by Richard Wright

Uncle Tom's Children: Four Novellas, 1938

Uncle Tom's Children: Five Long Stories, 1938

Native Son, 1940

"How "Bigger' Was Born," 1940.

Twelve Million Black Voices: A Folk History of the Negro in the U.S., 1941

Native Son (play, with Paul Green), 1941

Black Boy: A Record of Childhood and Youth, 1945

Native Son (screenplay), 1951

The Outsider, 1953.

Savage Holiday, 1954

Black Power: A Record of Reactions in a Land of Pathos, 1954

The Color Curtain: A Report on the Bandung Conference, 1956

Pagan Spain: A Report of a Journey into the Past, 1957

White Man, Listen!, 1957

The Long Dream, 1958

Quintet (editor, short stories), 1961.

Eight Men, 1961

Lawd Today, 1963

Letters to Joe C. Brown, 1968.

Daddy Goodness (play, with Louis Sapin), 1968.

The Man Who Lived Underground, 1971.

What the Negro Wants (contributor), 1972.

American Hunger, 1977.

The Richard Wright Reader, 1978.

Richard Wright: Works 2 vols., 1991

Conversations with Richard Wright, 1993.

Rite of Passage, 1994.

Haiku: This Other World, 1998.

Annotated Bibliography

Algeo, Ann M. *The Courtroom as Forum: Homicide Trials by Dreiser, Wright, Capote, and Mailer*. New York: Peter Lang, 1996.

In this volume Algeo assesses the book's final section, examining its language, message, and structure.

Baker, Houston A. *Twentieth Century Interpretations of* Native Son. Englewood Cliffs, NJ: Prentice-Hall, Inc., 1972.

This collection of early responses to Wright's novel include a number of landmark essays.

Bloom, Harold, ed. *Major Literary Characters: Bigger Thomas*. New York: Chelsea House Publishers, 1990.

Here, Bloom collects a series of essays debating the character of Bigger Thomas and what he represents.

Butler, Robert. Native Son: *The Emergence of a New Black Hero*. Boston: Twayne Publishers, 1991.

In this volume, Butler provides a background of the critical response and cultural contexts in addition to a straightforward assessment of techniques used in the fiction. He also includes a timeline and selected bibliography.

Carreiro, Amy E. "Ghosts of the Harlem Renaissance: "Negrotarians" in Richard Wright's *Native Son*." *The Journal of Negro History*, 84:3 (Summer 1999), pp. 247–259.

Carreiro offers a historical grounding for the Communist Party of the United States of America and the ways in which Wright's criticism of the CPUS and the reform movement led by whites manifests itself in the novel.

Ellis, Aimé J. "'Boys in the Hood': Black Male Community in Richard Wright's *Native Son*." *Callaloo* 29:1 (2006), pp.182–201.

Ellis elaborates on the creation of community within the novel, arguing that Bigger was more connected to his environment and his friends than other critics have acknowledged. He claims the friendship and the various hangouts as sites for emotional intimacy.

Fabre, Michael. *The World of Richard Wright*. Jackson: The University of Mississippi Press, 1985.

Fabre collects essays written over fifteen years to form this study of Wright and his work. Of particular interest is the essay "Fantasies and Style in Wright's Fiction" for its assessment of imagery and the subconscious.

Gates, Henry Louis, Jr. and K. A. Appiah, eds. *Richard Wright: Critical Perspectives Past and Present*. New York: Amistad Press, Inc., 1993.

This collection of scholarly essays, published between 1938 and 1992, examines Wright, his work, and his critical reception and legacy.

Guttman, Sondra. "What Bigger Killed For: Rereading Violence Against Women in *Native Son*." *Texas Studies in Language and Literature* (43:2), Summer 2001, pp. 169–193.

Guttman re-examines the feminist critique of women in Wright's fiction, adding smart commentary on race, class, and the sexualization of racism.

Hakutani, Yoshinobu. *Richard Wright and Racial Discourse*. Columbia: University of Missouri Press, 1996.

Hakuntani examines Wright's work as racial discourse, explaining the ways in which it expanded to encompass international concepts of race and the effects that discourse had on emerging writers.

Joyce, Joyce Ann. *Richard Wright's Art of Tragedy*. Iowa City: University of Iowa Press, 1986.

Here Joyce offers a close reading of *Native Son* which illustrates the thesis that the novel is a tragedy in the Aristotelian definition.

Kinnamon, Keneth. *New Essays on* Native Son. Cambridge: Cambridge University Press, 1990.

A small collection of four essays addressing Afro-American Literature, Afro-American Modernism, women, and narrative politics in the novel.

Kinnamon, Keneth. *The Emergence of Richard Wright: A Study in Literature and Society*. Urbana: University of Illinois Press, 1972.

Kinnamon intertwines biographical, social, and literary analysis to make sense of varying critical responses to Wright and his works. He offers easy to comprehend criticism of major themes, stylistic devices, and structures.

Kinnamon, Keneth, ed. *Critical Essays on Richard Wright's* Native Son. New York: Twayne Publishers, 1997.

Kinnamon includes early reviews and reprinted essays in addition to three essays written especially for the volume. It provides a useful compendium for evaluating critical comment over the decades.

Margolies, Edward. *The Art of Richard Wright*. Carbondale: Southern Illinois University Press, 1969.

Though Margolies refers to *Native Son* as "proletarian literature" and "transparently propagandistic," he offers a strong basic assessment of structure, technique, and plot in his chapter on the novel.

Miller, Eugene E. *Voice of a Native Son: The Poetics of Richard Wright*. Jackson: The University Press of Mississippi, 1990.

Miller's volume is a book-length examination of Wright's style and technique. Unlike many critics, Miller considers not only what is said in the works, but how it is said.

Miller, James A., ed. *Approaches to Teaching Wright's* Native Son. New York: The Modern Language Association of America, 1997.

This collection of essays establishes a number of different approaches to critically reading *Native Son*. The essays are generally short and very accessible.

Ray, David and Robert M. Farnsworth, eds. *Richard Wright: Impressions and Perspectives.* Ann Arbor: The University of Michigan Press, 1971.

These editors grouped essays based on geography and topic, providing letters as well as criticism. It also provides a useful bibliography compiled by Michael Fabre and Edward Margolies.

Savory, Jerold J. "Bigger Thomas and the Book of Job: The Epigraph to *Native Son.*" *Negro American Literary Forum*, 9:2 (Summer, 1975), pp. 55–56.

Savory offers an interesting reading of Bigger as a modern day Job.

Smethurst, James. "Invented by Horror: The Gothic and African American Literary Ideology in *Native Son. African American Review* 35:1 (Spring 2001), pp. 29–40.

Smethurst charts the influence of the Gothic through Wright's novel.

Tolentino, Cynthia. "The Road out of the Black Belt: Sociology's Fictions and Black Subjectivity in *Native Son.*" *NOVEL: A Forum on Fiction*, 33:3 (Summer 2000), pp. 377–405.

Tolentino looks at Wright's political assertion, in *Native Son*, that white liberalism, including Communism, leaves blacks with limited roles and agency. She provides both biographical and textual details to support her theory.

Contributors

Harold Bloom is Sterling Professor of the Humanities at Yale University. He is the author of 30 books, including *Shelley's Mythmaking*, *The Visionary Company*, *Blake's Apocalypse*, *Yeats*, *A Map of Misreading*, *Kabbalah and Criticism*, *Agon: Toward a Theory of Revisionism*, *The American Religion*, *The Western Canon*, and *Omens of Millennium: The Gnosis of Angels, Dreams, and Resurrection*. *The Anxiety of Influence* sets forth Professor Bloom's provocative theory of the literary relationships between the great writers and their predecessors. His most recent books include *Shakespeare: The Invention of the Human*, a 1998 National Book Award finalist, *How to Read and Why*, *Genius: A Mosaic of One Hundred Exemplary Creative Minds*, *Hamlet: Poem Unlimited*, *Where Shall Wisdom Be Found?*, and *Jesus and Yahweh: The Names Divine*. In 1999, Professor Bloom received the prestigious American Academy of Arts and Letters Gold Medal for Criticism. He has also received the International Prize of Catalonia, the Alfonso Reyes Prize of Mexico, and the Hans Christian Andersen Bicentennial Prize of Denmark.

Camille-Yvette Welsch teaches at the Pennsylvania State University. She is a poet and critic whose work has appeared in *Mid-American Review*, *The AWP Writer's Chronicle*, *The Women's Review of Books*, *Barrow Street*, and *Small Spiral Notebook*, among other venues.

Aimé J. Ellis is Assistant Professor of English at Michigan State University. He is currently working on his first book, *If We Must Die: From Bigger Thomas to Biggie Smalls*.

Michael Bérubé is Professor of English at the Pennsylvania State University. His many books include *What's Liberal About the Liberal Arts?: Classroom Politics and 'Bias' in Higher Education*, *Life As We Know It: A Father, a Family, and an Exceptional Child*, and *The Aesthetics of Cultural Studies*, among others.

Michael Fabre is Professor Emeritus at Paris-La Sorbonne. He is the author of *The Unfinished Quest of Richard Wright*, *From Harlem to Paris: Black American Writers in France, 1840 to 1980*, among other books, the editor of *Conversations with Chester Himes*, and the co-author of *The Several Lives of Chester Himes*.

Sondra Guttman has held appointments at Rutgers University and Ithaca College, and was Visiting Assistant Professor of American Literature at Concordia University in Montreal. Her latest project, *Looking for Little Sister: Sexual Violence and Social Change in Depression-Era American Fiction*, focuses on sexual violence during the Depression.

Farah Jasmine Griffin is Professor of English and Comparative Literature at Columbia University. She is the author of *If You Can't Be Free Be A Mystery: In Search of Billie Holiday* and *Who Set You Flowin'?: The African American Migration Narrative*, the co-editor of *Stranger in the Village: Two Centuries of African American Travel Writing*, and the editor of *Beloved Sisters and Loving Friends: Letters from Addie Brown and Rebecca Primus*.

Caren Irr is Associate Professor of English and American Literature at Brandeis University. She is the author of *The Suburb of Dissent: Cultural Politics in the United States and Canada During the 1930's* and the co-author of *Rethinking the Frankfurt School: Alternative Legacies of Cultural Critique* and *On Jameson: From Postmodernism to Globalization*.

Barbara Johnson is the Frederic Wertham Professor of Law and Psychiatry in Society in the Harvard University Department of Comparative Literature. She is the author of many books, including *Mother Tongues*, *The Feminist Difference: Literature, Psychoanalysis, Race, and Gender*, *The Wake of Deconstruction*, *A World of Difference*, and *The Critical Difference: Essays in the Contemporary Rhetoric of Reading*.

Kenneth Kinnamon is the Ethel Pumphrey Stephens Professor of English at the University of Arkansas. He is author of numerous articles on American literature, *The Emergence of Richard Wright: A Study of Literature and Society*, and *A Richard Wright Bibliography: Fifty Years of Criticism and Commentary, 1933–1982*. He has edited two books on James Baldwin and co-edited (with Richard Barksdale) *Black Writers of America: A Comprehensive Anthology*.

James Nagel is the Edison Distinguished Professor of English at the University of Georgia. He has edited several collections on the works of Ernest Hemingway, Stephen Crane, and Hamlin Garland, as well as the Penguin Twentieth-Century Classics edition of John Steinbeck's *Pastures of Heaven*.

Ross Pudaloff is an Associate Professor at Wayne State University. He is the author of *Witchcraft at Salem: (Mis)representing the Subject*; *Education and the Constitution: Instituting American Culture, Celebrity as Identity: Richard Wright, Native Son, and Mass Culture*; *Thoreau's Composition of the Narrator: From Sexuality to Language;* and *A Boundless Duration Before You: Edwards at Enfield, 1741*.

James Smethurst is Assistant Professor in the W.E.B. Du Bois Department of Afro-American Studies at the University of Massachusetts-Amherst. He is the co-editor of *Left of the Color Line: Race, Radicalism, and Twentieth-Century Literature of the United States*. He is author of *The New Red Negro: The Literary Left and African-American Poetry, 1930–1946*.

Craig Werner is Professor of African-American Studies at the University of Wisconsin, where he teaches courses on Black Music and American Cultural History. He is the author of *A Change is Gonna Come: Music, Race, and the Soul of America*.

Yoshinobu Hakutani is a Professor of English at Kent State. He had edited a number of books, including Richard Wright's *Haiku: This Other World* and *Postmodernity and Cross Culturalism*, among others. He is also the author of a number of articles on Richard Wright.

Joyce Ann Joyce taught at Chicago State University where she was Professor of English, Associate Director of the Gwendolyn Brooks Center, the chairperson of the Black Studies Department, and coordinator of the Honors Program. She also served as chairperson and professor of the African-American Studies Department at Temple University. Her books include *Warriors, Conjurers, and Priests: Defining African-centered Literary Criticism* and *Sonia Sanchez and the African Poetic Tradition.*

Acknowledgments

Ellis, Aimé J. "'Boys in the Hood': Black Male Community in Richard Wright's *Native Son*." *Callaloo* 29:1 (2006), pp.189–191.

Bérubé, Michael. "Max, Media, and Mimesis: Bigger's Representation in *Native Son*." *Approaches to Teaching Wright's* Native Son. James A. Miller, ed. New York: The Modern Language Association of America, 1997, pp. 112–115.

Fabre, Michael. "Fantasies and Style in Wright's Fiction." *The World of Richard Wright*. Jackson: The University of Mississippi Press, 1985, pp. 128–130.

Guttman, Sondra. "What Bigger Killed For: Rereading Violence Against Women in *Native Son*." *Texas Studies in Language and Literature* (43:2), Summer 2001, pp. 178–179.

Griffin, Farah Jasmine. "On Women, Teaching, and *Native Son*." *Approaches to Teaching Wright's* Native Son. James A. Miller, ed. New York: The Modern Language Association of America, 1997, pp. 78–80.

Irr, Caren. "The Politics of Spatial Phobias in *Native Son*." *Critical Essays on Richard Wright's* Native Son. Keneth Kinnamon, ed. New York: Twayne Publishers, 1997, pp. 199–201.

Johnson, Barbara. "The Re(a)d and the Black." *Richard Wright: Critical Perspectives Past and Present*. Gates, Henry Louis, Jr. and K. A. Appiah, eds. New York: Amistad Press, Inc., 1993, pp. 149–152.

Kinnamon, Keneth. "How Native Son Was Born." *Richard Wright: Critical Perspectives Past and Present*. Gates, Henry Louis, Jr. and K. A. Appiah, eds. New York: Amistad Press, Inc., 1993, pp. 122–125.

Nagel, James. "Images of 'Vision' in *Native Son. Critical Essays on Richard Wright's* Native Son. Keneth Kinnamon, ed. New York: Twayne Publishers, 1997, pp. 86– 89.

Pudaloff, Ross. "Celebrity as Identity: *Native Son* and Mass Culture." *Richard Wright: Critical Perspectives Past and Present.* Gates, Henry Louis, Jr. and K. A. Appiah, eds. New York: Amistad Press, Inc., 1993, pp. 161–163.

Smethurst, James. "Invented by Horror: The Gothic and African American Literary Ideology in *Native Son. African American Review* 35:1 (Spring 2001), pp. 33–34.

Werner, Craig. "Bigger's Blues: *Native Son* and the Articulation of Afro-American Modernism." *New Essays on* Native Son. Cambridge: Cambridge University Press, 1990, pp. 128–132.

Hakutani, Yoshinobu. "*Native Son* and American Culture." *Richard Wright and Racial Discourse.* Columbia: University of Missouri Press, 1996, pp. 78–80.

Joyce, Joyce Ann. "Technique." *Richard Wright's Art of Tragedy.* Iowa City: University of Iowa Press, 1986, pp. 80–83.

Index

Characters in literary works are indexed by first name (if any), followed by the name of the work in parentheses